ALL THE DAYS
OF MY LIFE

Recollections of
Herbert W. Dickson
as told to
Jean S. Corbett

ALL THE DAYS OF MY LIFE

Recollections of
Herbert W. Dickson
as told to
Jean S. Corbett

"Surely goodness and mercy shall follow me
ALL THE DAYS OF MY LIFE:
and I will dwell in the house of the Lord for ever."
Psalm 23:6

A QUA IBOE MISSION PUBLICATION

© Jean S. Corbett

First published 1981

ISBN 0 950 7657 0 8

Published by
Qua Iboe Mission
7 Donegall Square West
Belfast BT1 6JE
North Ireland

Printed in Great Britain

Contents

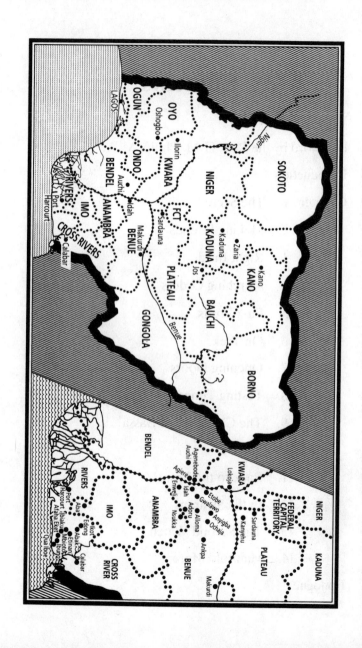

Foreword

by Rev. George M. Philip,
Sandyford-Henderson Memorial Church, Glasgow.

Twenty-five years ago, as a young minister recently inducted to his first charge, I preached one morning a solemn message on Judgment. It was not easy, for few understood or sympathised with the Gospel. Unknown to me, Herbert Dickson was in the congregation because he lived within walking distance of the church. Early in the following week I received a letter from him saying he had been there, expressing how much he understood the cost of preaching the truth faithfully, assuring me of his prayers and saying he would worship with us whenever he could.

That began a valued friendship and partnership in the Gospel, which forged strong and precious bonds between Herbert Dickson and our fellowship. It is an incident which, to me, highlights one of his great characteristics. He has always been a man who encouraged others to be faithful to God, to trust God and to go on with God no matter the circumstances. How clearly I can recall him saying, "The Lord never said it would be easy." There was a realism about him, as well as an outgoing spirit of care that made people, including children, feel wanted and valued. There was no false piety about him when he spoke of the privilege of serving the Lord, and there was something infectious about his oft-repeated phrase, "Who wouldn't be a missionary?"

No one in our prayer meeting will ever forget the night he spoke to us (and there were many heart-warming times) on the verse, *"My glory I will not give to another."* He spoke of his great burden to see some of the old men of the villages come to Christ before he left for home. But none came. Then, he said, when Herbert Dickson was out of the way and back to Scotland, news began to come of some of the men being converted. He was happy that it should be so. His concern was always to point people to Christ, not to Herbert Dickson.

The fifty years and more of this missionary's life and work is a story to be read carefully. He does not say much about the privation or difficulties or disappointments. The Nigeria he went to, at the beginning, was very different from the one he left, but in all the changes he never lost sight of the fact that, in Africa or Britain, the need of man is met only in Christ. The Jesus Christ he preached by lip and life was the Son of God who loved him and gave himself for him.

This is Herbert Dickson's theme: the privilege of serving Christ. He never liked fuss but was deeply moved by the love the people had for him. He is a man greatly loved. If we wrote of the trumpets sounding for him, he would be rather embarrassed. He would prefer to think that the best use for a crown is to lay it at Jesus' feet.

Read the story and let God thrill and challenge your heart. If it stirs your interest, makes you pray, and quickens your desire to give your life to serve Christ, long-term rather than short-term, whether in Nigeria or any other part of the world, Herbert Dickson will feel his work well done.

Introduction

As one of "Uncle Herbie's" adopted nieces within the Qua Iboe Family, it has been an education and a challenge to work with him in the preparation of this book. We have tried to tell the story in his own words and way, but it is not easy to capture in cold print the infectious enthusiasm and sense of fun, or the single-minded devotion and warmth of personality that have made Herbert Dickson a legend in his own lifetime.

No one could have been more co-operative but, again and again he would say,

"We mustn't make it sound as if I was the only one. Others were involved and should be mentioned too."

"But," I would reason, "if there are too many names the readers will be confused and lose the thread of the story."

We agreed to compromise, so may I ask for patience from friends who notice omissions, as well as from more casual readers who may feel there is too much detail?

To my great regret, Mr. Dickson has not been able to check the completed manuscript as he became ill soon after supplying material for the final chapters. We are deeply thankful that the work was so far advanced and pray that these recollections of God's goodness may bring glory to the name of Christ and encouragement to his people everywhere.

Jean S. Corbett

CHAPTER ONE

The Secret

"Ladies and gentlemen, we are now approaching the international airport at Kano. We hope you have had a pleasant journey. Please fasten your seat belts and prepare for landing. Thank you."

Below us lay the ancient Muslim city with its mosques and minarets, its huge pyramids of ground nuts and famous indigo dye pits. The big Sabena 'plane taxied smoothly along the runway and soon we emerged into the blinding heat of northern Nigeria. On the tarmac stood a group of men with beaming faces and outstretched hands. The leaders of the Qua Iboe church in Kano had come to welcome the representatives of the Qua Iboe Mission on their anniversary visit and guide them safely through immigration and customs to the comfortable airport hotel.

Time was short and, promising to return, we set off again next morning in a smaller aircraft of Nigerian Airways. Beneath us now there stretched a panorama of sunbaked earth, dry river beds and clusters of small dwellings among sparse vegetation. Strange to be able to trace the entire course of a road or river at one glance, when at ground level one could only see as far as the next bend!

The unfolding scene matched my mood as I thought back over a life of more than fourscore years. At many a bend I had wondered what lay ahead but, even before I knew him, my heavenly Father had been mapping out the route and guiding my steps from his vantage point of eternity.

I was born into a humble family in Port Glasgow on the river Clyde on 15th October 1894. My parents, David and Rebecca Dickson, were a godly pair. Father was a shipbuilder by trade. He was also a preacher of the Gospel, with a good voice for speaking in the open-air. As well as being a faithful member of the United Free Church of Scotland, he had founded an evangelical Mission in Shore Street, where many people were converted to Christ.

Mother was a gentle, saintly woman who surrounded us with love. Undoubtedly her Christlike life in our home played a great part in bringing her children, one by one, to trust her Saviour. I was seventh in the family of ten, but knew only three brothers and four sisters, as the twins born before me had died at seven and thirteen months respectively.

As a result of illness I became blind when just over a year old and for many months was carried every day for treatment at the Eye Infirmary in Greenock. I don't remember the actual blindness but clearly recall, as a small boy, the regular visits to the Infirmary, and the green eyeshades and darkened rooms to protect my weakened sight. This treatment cost many precious weeks of schooling each year. Nevertheless I managed to enter Senior Primary School at the usual age and to complete the 4th year there before being taken away to help supplement the family income. Two years later, at the age of sixteen, I became an apprentice plater in Russell and Company's shipyard – now owned by Scott Lithgow.

The outbreak of world war in August 1914 was quickly followed by very heavy losses of medical personnel and an S.O.S. went out for men with some First Aid training. By this time I had obtained a St. Andrew's Medallion in First Aid and, with six other members of the Shipyard Ambulance Corps, immediately volunteered to serve with the Royal Army Medical Corps. It was 15th September 1914, six weeks after the declaration of war and one month before my twentieth birthday. The very next day we were sent to the R.A.M.C. depot at Aldershot.

After a few weeks intensive drilling, our seven recruits were scattered to various posts. I was sent to a military hospital near Portsmouth for nursing training which lasted till the following May, when I landed in France as part of the 20th. General Hospital. Our first task was the erection of a hospital under canvas at Dannes Camiers, not far from Etaples, where I became orderly-in-charge of a surgical ward with thirty-six beds. Two nursing sisters and one general duty orderly completed the ward staff. It was there, at 20th. General Hospital, that the course of my life was dramatically changed.

The arrival of mail from home was always a big event and one morning I was thrilled to receive a good-sized parcel. It was afternoon before I had time to open it, but through the hours of grim duties I speculated on what it might contain. At last I was free. One by one the items were carefully unpacked and laid out, all very acceptable additions to our monotonous rations. Now I must write and thank the kind friends who had packed it with such loving care. There was just one snag. Tucked in between the tins was a little booklet, which I knew had not got there by accident. It would be impossible to thank these folk without being able to add, "I read the tract too." The best thing would be to read it once and get it out of sight before my pals came off duty and began to rag me.

Stretching out on the narrow wooden bed I reluctantly opened the tract. It was called "Armageddon". I smiled knowingly. Familiar stuff;

13

quite unrelated to life on the western front. Or was it? All around me lay horrifying evidences of man's suffering and sin. Danger was never far away. Death was a stark reality. It wasn't hard to picture that final conflict between good and evil, and the coming Judgement of men and nations. In spite of my Christian background and clean living I knew I wasn't ready to meet God.

As a child I had been taught the way of salvation by parents, Sunday School teachers and preachers. I was about ten years old when evangelist, William Thompson came to conduct a mission in Port Glasgow. Using slides on the Pilgrim's Progress, he made the Gospel very plain and the whole town seemed to come alive to Christ. With hundreds of other children, wee Herbie Dickson decided to start on the pilgrim pathway. Alas, he had made little progress and young manhood brought no confirmation of that first step.

The memory of those days came flooding back – the warnings and prayers of my parents, the football and rowing friends with whom my time had been spent, the cardplaying and gambling that claimed my devotion. Often I had been afraid of being cut off suddenly, but never before had I trembled under waves of conviction such as broke upon me now.

There was only one thing to be done. On my knees before the Lord I made full confession of my waywardness and committed my life into his keeping. The great transaction was done! Without delay I got out pen and paper and wrote to my parents, and to a fellow footballer in another regiment, telling them what had taken place. Before long the news would reach all my pals. The boats were burned. There could be no going back.

That was February 16th 1916. Soon afterwards I

was transferred to the 14th Field Ambulance, stationed behind the Arras Front. There, within sight and sound of enemy action, another orderly and I began work in an emergency operating theatre. Under some of Britain's top surgeons, I was taught to give anaesthetics with ether and chloroform, and learned a lot about surgery. Little did I imagine how useful this experience would be in future years!

My next move was to the Somme, where some sixty thousand British lads, many from an Ulster regiment, were mown down in the first day's battle. At our "walking wounded" post we were responsible for treating our own men and prisoners alike, and how thankful I was to have the presence and peace of God in my heart during those awful days.

Enemy submarines had been causing heavy shipping losses, so in 1917, in company with many other skilled workers, I was called back to the shipyard. As a fully-fledged plater working overtime, I was now earning up to fourteen pounds per week, a big wage for those days. It was satisfying to be able to give substantial help in the home and to Christian work at home and abroad. While on leave I had testified to my new-found faith and now began to help in Shore Street Mission. I also taught a Sunday School class and attended the Christian Endeavour Society in the local Baptist church. These activities kept me busy and led to invitations to speak at mission halls in the surrounding district.

Overseas missions interested me and I was often moved when listening to speakers from the Regions Beyond Missionary Union, Sudan United Mission and Qua Iboe Mission. Two men had particularly impressed me, David Forbes of S.U.M., who came from Port Glasgow, and R.L. McKeown, General Secretary of the Belfast-based Qua Iboe Mission. As

15

they spoke of the urgent need for workers I sensed the call of God and a violent struggle began in my heart. Had I not done my bit? Was I not entitled to a more comfortable life? Could I not help by sending others? As I put up all these arguments I began to realise the grip that money was getting upon me. All joy in prayer and study of God's word was lost as he faced me with the challenge, "Don't speak to me when you won't obey me."

I was utterly miserable and unable to share my problem with anyone. Then one day at work I became suddenly ill. Next morning I was no better and the doctor was summoned. After examining me he left, saying he would be back soon. Who did he return with but the Sanitary Inspector!

"Scarlet fever", they announced, "and we want to know where you got it. There's not another case in the country."

What could I say? I did not know where I had got it and if I had told them *why* they would have thought I was raving! Like Jonah, I had been trying to run away from God, and he needed to take drastic measures to get me back on the right road.

At that time scarlet fever was a notifiable disease, involving four weeks quarantine. As mine was an isolated case, the doctor agreed that I could be nursed at home by my mother, who must be my only visitor. After a few days' sickness I felt quite well, and there in the quietness of my bedroom God met with me. By the help of his Holy Spirit I was able to say from my heart, "Lord, here am I. Show me where you want me to go."

Having got thus far I could hardly wait to discover the next step, but how, in that small room, could God reveal his plan and purpose? One day the R.B.M.U. magazine arrived, soon followed by that of the Sudan

United Mission. Both were read eagerly from cover to cover. They were interesting, but brought no special guidance. Then one morning my mother laid another modest publication on my bed.

"That's the Qua Iboe Quarterly Paper," she said.

Opening it with prayer in my heart, I read about a recent survey of unoccupied territories to the west and north of the Qua Iboe area of West Africa. The Mission's statement concluded: "To maintain the existing work and to enter these territories, at least eight new men are needed. The Empire counted no sacrifice too great – giving its noblest to win through in the fearful struggle of the past four years. The voice of One who has redeemed the world speaks to us, through the confusion of war's sad aftermath, of his unfinished work."

As clearly as the words of my mother, that other voice spoke to my heart saying, "You are to be one of the eight."

The message was so unmistakable that as soon as I was released from quarantine I wrote to the Belfast headquarters of the Qua Iboe Mission, and at the same time applied for admission as a student at the Bible Training Institute in Glasgow. The Mission's reply was non-committal: "You can let us know when your B.T.I. course is finished." They knew that many a call does not survive the test of time and training, and indeed there were to be periods of doubt which would cast me more and more upon the Lord.

In the Bible Training Institute, in those days, there was a deeply spiritual atmosphere and I was one of five students who formed a habit of meeting every Friday for a half-night of prayer in preparation for the weekend services. We were all longing for God's blessing on our lives and sometimes discussed the filling of the Holy Spirit, which some claimed to have

17

experienced, but about which others, including myself, were inclined to be sceptical. Back in my own room after one of these sessions, I faced the issue on my knees, determined to settle it once and for all.

"Lord, if you have anything to show me, please make it plain," I prayed. "If there is anything hindering your fulness in my life, search it out and make me willing to have done with it."

I do not know how long I remained there in the quietness, my heart wide open before my Lord. At last a neglected duty began to loom large. It seemed too insignificant to matter so I kept waiting for further light. None came, but the conviction strengthened, until at last I said,

"Lord, if this thing is holding back your blessing, I here and now give my word that it will be put right and never neglected again. Now, Lord – your answer?"

Like a flash, God reminded me that, as I had trusted his word about forgiveness through the Lord Jesus, so now I must do the same with his promise, *"If ye then being evil, know how to give good gifts unto your children, how much more shall your heavenly Father give the Holy Spirit to those that ask him?"* Knowing that the Holy Spirit was already in my heart, I simply asked,

"Lord, fill me and use me for your glory."

There were no dramatic signs from heaven, but I lay down to rest with great peace of mind that God had heard and answered prayer. Next morning this assurance was still so real that I shared it with the other students gathered in the big sitting room before going off to our weekend assignments. Did it last? Well, many a time I have grieved the Holy Spirit and lost the wonderful joy, but I soon learned to get back immediately to the Lord to set matters right. Having

18

once tasted the sweetness of close fellowship with him, how could I allow anything to come between us again?

To my great surprise, in my second year at B.T.I., I was chosen as students' chairman. This brought experience in dealing with personalities and circumstances, which proved very useful in the lifework which lay ahead. As yet I had told no one of my conviction that I was to be one of the eight. That was a secret between God and me. From time to time, news was given of another young man accepted by the Qua Iboe Mission. I lost count of them and was afraid to enquire, but it became desperately important that I should be included in that particular group. If I had been mistaken about God's message, how could I ever be sure about anything again?

Halfway through my final year of studies I applied to the Mission and was summoned to Belfast for interview during the Easter vacation. Crossing by the night steamer, I reached the home of the General Secretary in time for breakfast. When the meal was over and the children off to school, Mr. McKeown sat by the fireside putting on his boots in readiness for another busy day in the office.

"Well, Herbert," he said, "you'll be free till the Council meeting at five o'clock, so enjoy the day looking round Belfast."

Enjoy the day! Little did he know how I was feeling. Dare I ask my burning question? I hesitated. The General Secretary was a kindly man but he might get a bad impression if the new candidate was too curious or betrayed his pent-up emotions. On the other hand, how could I endure another eight hours' suspense?

Summoning up my courage, and in as matter-of-fact a tone as I could muster, I ventured,

"Mr. McKeown, some years ago the Mission appealed for eight young men. Have you got them yet?"

"R.L.", as he was affectionately known in the Mission family, stopped lacing his boots and looked up. He began to count on his fingers,

"One...two...three...four...five...six...seven..."

He paused. I held my breath.

"If you are accepted tonight, you'll be the eighth," he said.

Four months later I was in Nigeria. After being accepted by Council, I had completed my term at B.T.I., gathered a basic tropical kit and set off from home amid the prayers and blessings of my family and friends. The three weeks' sea journey ended at Calabar on 4th August 1922. From that historic port the small steamer, Geo. Watts, carried me along the coastline, across the bar and up the winding Qua Iboe river to the trading centre of Eket. Here, at the Girls' Institute, I was welcomed into the Mission family and spent my first night under a mosquito net, surrounded by the humid heat and strange noises of the African bush.

Next morning I was up early, ready for the last stage of the journey to Mbioto, where I was expected to take over from a missionary who was soon due for furlough. Just before leaving Scotland I had learned to ride a motorcycle and gladly accepted the offer of one with a side-car for use in Nigeria. The side-car seemed a good idea. The extra wheel would make me feel safer and it could accommodate an African helper and the camping gear needed on safari. This outfit had accompanied me on the steamer and was now to carry me to my new home.

My guide was a young missionary, also one of the eight, who already knew the way and would go ahead

20

on his own motorbike. All I had to do was follow. Speeding along the narrow sandy roads everything seemed fine and I was thrilled to be in Africa. Then I began to realise what was happening. As the first engine roared past, men, women and children were flocking out of nowhere to gaze at the departing cloud of dust. They did not know that a second cyclist was following, and an inexperienced one at that. Again and again I had to slow down to avoid an accident. By then my guide would be out of sight and I was forced to accelerate to catch up with him. It wasn't only the unaccustomed tropical heat that caused the perspiration to flow freely that day!

The sun was beginning to set and, having been warned how brief would be the twilight, I was anxious to reduce the distance between us. The people scattered. To my horror I saw ahead of me, not the expected clear road, but a narrow strip of cement and beyond it the Qua Iboe river! On the pontoon, which the current had already pulled down-stream, sat my terror-stricken friend and his motorbike. Before me, only eight feet away, lay the open river, with absolutely nothing to save me from a watery grave.

But God had not brought me to Nigeria to drown before even reaching my location or speaking a word for him. Clutching both handlebars with all my strength, I instinctively stood upright. Miraculously, the cycle stopped with its front wheel about six inches over the edge of the cement platform. By grasping the handlebars I had opened the clutch and put on the handbrake. At the same time, by standing up, my whole weight had been thrown on the footbrake. Without realising it, I had been guided to take the right action.

As for my friend on the pontoon, he could see nothing for me but the river and was violently sick with shock, not only there but again when we eventually reached our destination! This incident taught me a lesson. God expects us to use the commonsense and faculties he has given us. When the situation gets beyond us he will step in to safeguard his will and purpose.

All that happened fifty-six years ago. Now here I was, in October 1978, surveying the land that had become my second home. Beside me in the 'plane sat a new General Secretary of the Qua Iboe Mission and we were on our way to represent Home Council at anniversary services of the Qua Iboe Church. Was it any wonder that my heart was full of praise to the great God who had guided and guarded every step of my pilgrim pathway to that very hour?

CHAPTER TWO

Making Friends

The old church at Ibeno was bursting at the seams with a colourful crowd of people, dressed in their Sunday best. Hundreds more were seated outside under palm leaf shelters which provided some shade from the strong rays of the sun. A year previously, the 90th anniversary of the Qua Iboe Mission had been celebrated in a thanksgiving rally in Belfast and now it was the turn of the Qua Iboe Church to give thanks to God for the coming of the Gospel in 1887.

A booklet had been prepared, recalling the early days when Samuel Bill, alone and without human resources, had brought the Good News to Ibeno. From there the message had spread northwards until now there were over nine hundred and fifty congregations in the self-governing, self-supporting and self-propagating Qua Iboe Church. What a privilege to have had a share in such a work of God!

After the reading of this official record and numerous other addresses, Pastor Amos Udonsak, Principal of the Q.I.C. Bible College, called on me to convey the greetings of Home Council. His introduction outlined the service my wife and I had given in various locations.

"And what's more," he concluded, to my further embarrassment, "this is his birthday. He's eighty-four today!"

Well, with that the congregation exploded into excited exclamations, necks craning in all directions to see this ancient wonder! At the close of the service there were many old friends to greet, but no reunion brought greater joy than that with William Usen, the frail senior pastor of Ibeno and of the whole Qua Iboe Church. The story of our friendship spans well over fifty years.

After arriving in Mbioto in September 1922, I had just a month with the missionary there, before being left with the oversight of eighty-four churches. In those days the preacher was usually the only literate person in the village and, as well as preaching and pastoral duties, he had to teach adults and children to read the word of God. Supervision of these literacy classes and Standard IV primary schools formed part of my responsibility and one of the preacher-teachers, William Usen, was appointed to be my interpreter and helper in this unfamiliar task.

William was a few years younger than myself and proved to be a very congenial companion. He had a happy nature and loved to sing, indeed he was commonly known by his other name, Iquo, which means "song". In all the years of our association, I don't think I ever saw him angry. A house was built on the Mission compound and William lived here with his quiet, unassuming wife and three small daughters, who soon became my friends. I can still picture the little curly-haired toddler crawling up the wooden steps to my house to greet the white man – and she was at Ibeno, with her father and sister, to welcome me back in 1978.

Having been brought up under the guidance of the Mission's founder, William Usen was able to keep me right in many problems involving local customs, church practice and discipline. The churches of Mbioto district were grouped together around thirteen centres where communion was observed quarterly. Every Sunday we would set out by bicycle, motorcycle or canoe, for one of other of these places. Prior to the communion, local churches were visited and at the same time the schools were contacted, as government regulations required the missionary-manager to inspect and sign the register each quarter.

One of our early visits was to Ibiaku area. We set off by motorbike and then trekked the final four miles to our destination. As we passed one village, William asked the church people to prepare some food for our return. When we got back a great welcome awaited us. A little table, about eighteen inches square, was set before us and on it a huge basin heaped with meat and yam, which was a sort of very large potato. I began cautiously, still unaccustomed to African food and aware that the protein could consist of animals which are unpleasant to a European. William was sensitive to the situation and poked through the pile, pushing some portions over to my side of the basin. I was relieved to find they were chicken and was soon enjoying a hearty meal. When we were satisfied, there was still plenty left for other people waiting their turn in the back yard!

During the meal, the open door and windows had been crowded with onlookers, for a white visitor was a rarity in that area. They were still there as we sat waiting to talk with the church leaders. A wooden bench was brought in and placed against the wall beside me. But the group that filed in to sit on it were not the expected men, but six belles of the village, aged about 15–18 years.

To hide my embarrassment I busied myself with a magazine I had brought with me, all the time wondering what the next move might be. After ten minutes they rose and quietly walked out, but my relief was short-lived as a similar group took their place on the bench. When this had gone on for some time I ventured to ask William,

"Do these young ladies want to ask me something?"

Bursting into hilarious laughter, William replied,

"Oh no, Etubom,* they only want a closer look at you!"

Then seeing that this had not eased my discomfort, he added reassuringly,

"Don't be annoyed, Etubom. I heard them say, 'Isn't he a lovely young man?' "

Such were the situations that faced a young missionary during his introduction to an unfamiliar culture. He would just have to get used to every movement being closely observed with uninhibited curiosity. And obviously a sense of humour was going to be a great asset!

In 1923 there was still much inter-tribal hostility and the government sometimes had to intervene with stern measures to subdue the lawbreakers. As a result, people feared to enter alien territory and there were many places to which the message of God's love had not yet penetrated.

One day a preacher called Sambo arrived from a distant village to consult William Usen. After talking together the two men sought me out, and William introduced Sambo's errand.

"Etubom," he said, "we have a heavy load on our minds about a people who have never heard of Jesus. Just lately a few young men from that tribe came to ask Sambo if you would be willing to take them this word of God that has changed so many of our people. We know you came to our country for this purpose but the Annang tribe is known to be very wild. No one from other tribes passes through their land. Even we would not go there, and yet Jesus died for them too. What can we do about this? Would you be afraid

*Efik name for 'Captain' or 'Master', given to white men.

26

to go?"

"No, William,' I replied," I wouldn't be afraid to go anywhere if God sends me. But we must ask him to show us when and how to approach them, so as to be accepted."

"Etubom," said Sambo, anxious that I should know the full story, "before you decide, we must tell you all we know about these people and their customs. They are cannibals and practice slavery and human sacrifice. They have told us that strangers who enter their area might not be heard of again. Even the government official with armed policemen has no control over them so you would have no protection. There could be a risk to your life and those who would accompany you."

Looking at the earnest faces, I realised something of the conflict in the minds of these good men.

"Thank you, dear friends, for telling me all this. Now let me remind you of God's side. We don't go alone. The Lord who gives the command also promises to be with his messengers. He says, *'I will build my Church and the gates of hell shall not prevail against it.'* There are stones for that building among the Annangs. Our Lord can deliver them from the stronghold of Satan and fit them into his building."

The day came when, under the guidance of God, we set out for Ikot Idem. After spending the night on the way we eventually reached our destination and it was obvious that my presence caused some excitement. As night drew on I was anxious to find a place to sleep and was given a small house, about eight feet square, without door or window frames.

It was now dark and I was very hungry. William and Sambo had gone off to look for food and lodging, and I had resigned myself to going supperless to bed when a few people arrived, one holding a storm lamp

27

and another a bucket containing a good supply of stew. It was placed before me with a smile, and I was given an enamel plate and spoon. A friendly hand held the lamp to help me see what I was spooning from the bucket, but when the paraffin began dropping I decided to dig in the dark! I was truly grateful for that stew.

All this time every movement was being watched, and I had a most attentive audience until I slipped under the mosquito net for the night. It was very dark and eerie in that open house. Mindful of all my helpers had told me, I committed myself and them into our heavenly Father's hands, turned over, and fell fast asleep. When I awoke next morning, the window and door were already crowded with eager spectators. I struggled to get dressed under the sheet and there was obvious surprise and disappointment when the young white man suddenly arose fully clothed!

The atmosphere in the town was tense and excited. We could not understand this, but thought it wiser not to attempt a public meeting. After talking with the young men who had invited us we set off for home, content to have made a first contact without opposition. The sound of a motorbike made us stop to see who could be arriving in this unlikely place. Along came a government officer whom I had met on a previous occasion.

"Where have you been?" he enquired, and when our errand was explained he exclaimed, "I'm relieved to see you safely out of it!"

He went on to tell us about several murders committed there some days before. African police sent to investigate had also been killed and now he had come prepared to deal with the offenders. This explained the tense atmosphere! No doubt I had been mistaken for the government officer by all but the few who knew our real mission. God had watched over us, even when we were unaware of danger.

That town was burned down in punishment for the killings. When it was rebuilt a preacher was stationed there and the word of God spread throughout the whole area, including what is now Ibesit district. How true it is that grace can do a deeper work than law alone can ever accomplish!

In 1923, the Mission had no doctor or hospital but every missionary was granted a permit to conduct a dispensary for the treatment of common ailments. Having learned of my R.A.M.C. experience, Mr. Bill must have looked on me as some sort of substitute for the only son whom he had hoped would become a missionary doctor, had he not been killed in action some years previously.

One day a group of people arrived at my house with a letter. It concerned a boy of twelve years who had been bitten on the foot by a snake. In their efforts to save his life, his family had caused the loss of his foot and gangrene had set in. Mr. Bill suggested that if I could amputate the remainder of the leg at the knee the boy's life might yet be saved.

Now I was ready to tackle most things but this seemed too much. True, I had helped at many amputations, but only in an operating theatre with skilled assistance, and surgeons to accept the responsibility. Here I would be on my own. At the same time I did not want to lose face with the Founder, and undoubtedly a life was at stake. Thinking to dissuade the parents, I described to them the details and dangers of the operation. No good! Having discussed it they concluded,

"We agree for you to do it."

There was no escape, and as the news spread

·excitement increased. Everyone wanted to see the first-ever operation under anaesthetic to be carried out in Qua Iboe. I decided for a day when there was a special service in the church which most people would be attending, and at the same time arranged for one of our missionary nurses to assist me. Her name was Hilda Davis.

Before leaving for Nigeria I had been able to purchase from the army a cabinet of surgical instruments and a case of equipment used in emergencies in the trenches, including chloroform and other items required for minor surgery. All was set out on the verandah of the Mission house, about eight feet above ground level, and the door was locked to avoid interruption.

I asked the nurse to give the anaesthetic but she was afraid to take the risk; however, she did hold the mask while I administered the chloroform. All went well with the amputation and the boy was soon lying on a bamboo bed. I opened the door for the mother to enter. At first she was very frightened to see her boy asleep and the bandage-swathed stump of his leg. When he opened his eyes she wanted to take him on her knee, but with a smile he clung to me and would go to no one else. The poor woman must have felt sure I had bewitched her son! As he still held me round the neck I got her to come nearer and, talking playfully to him, loosed his hands and slipped him on to her lap. Some days afterwards his people took him home and I later learned he was doing well and moving around with a crutch.

Contacts in the dispensary were opening many doors for the word and teaching me how to communicate with the people. At the same time I was trying to pass on to my young helper, Okon, some basic rules of hygiene and treatment.

"No, Okon, not that bottle. The one nearer the end of the shelf. Yes, the one with the yellow label. Tell the mother she must not use any other spoon than this small one I'm giving her. One spoonful at the time when people leave the house to go to market; one when the sun has passed the middle of the sky, and one just after the sun has going out of sight. Does she understand?"

"Yes, Etubom. These times are well known to her."

"Walk softly, mother. God bless you and make your baby recover soon. Don't forget the word of God you have heard this morning."

"Thank you, white man. You have taken the pain from my head and I can look at my child now without fear. The journey back to my village will be shorter than the journey to see you."

As we worked I had noticed a group of young men standing for a long time outside the dispensary. Okon told me they were not patients but waiting to speak to me, so, as usual, Evangelist William was summoned to help in the interview.

"Do you know these people, William?"

"No, Etubom. I've heard the name of their town but have never been there. They have come to beg you to visit them. The little group of Christians feel they are forgotten and of no account. Ikot Ekpung is difficult to reach and no white man has ever been there."

Pioneering was in my blood so we decided to accept the invitation and the delegation went away, very happy to bring news of the coming visit. Alas, when the appointed day came I was in bed with malaria and could not go. A few days later the men arrived to find out why I had not kept my word. When told of my illness they sympathised and a new

31

date was arranged. Can you imagine how I felt when, on this second occasion, I was again down with malaria? The delegation duly returned and, while believing our explanation, it was plain that they thought I was not really anxious to come. We tried to reassure them and fixed a third date.

Now what will you think when I tell you that this third date found me again in the grip of fever? I could see that William was as disappointed as I was, for this visit had been much in our prayers. Was the devil trying to stop us going, so that he could convince those believers that God had forgotten them too? I determined that, come what may, I was going to attempt the journey.

Carriers had already gone ahead with the camp equipment and we were to follow by bicycle, so, still shaking with fever, I mounted and set off. After six miles I could go no further and lay down at the roadside feeling very ill. William stood by, wondering if the end was near, while I cried to the Lord for renewed strength. Fifteen minutes later I was again on my cycle.

The journey seemed endless, but at last we reached a church at the edge of the forest where a crowd was waiting to greet us. I lay down in the preacher's house, exhausted, and realising that our destination was still a long way off. The young men from the "forgotten village" wanted to carry me, but I did not want to give in to this, so after a rest we set off again on foot, leaving our cycles behind as they would be no use in the remainder of the journey.

A mile or so into the forest we came to a long stretch of waist-deep water. Before I had time to step in, I was hoisted on to big strong shoulders and carried through to the other side. On we trudged, the determined effort making me perspire profusely and helping to relieve the fever. The problem now was agonising thirst. But where could I get anything to drink, as our supplies had gone before us to the village? The resourceful William spotted a man coming through the forest with a small calabash and found he had been tapping a palm wine tree. We don't encourage Christians to drink this wine, which can be very potent when fermented. Knowing this, William timidly asked would I be willing to take it. I replied I would drink anything at that moment and was handed the calabash. My, it was like nectar and fairly put me on my feet!

By this time the village had news of my arrival and chiefs and people, drummers and trumpets, all turned out to greet me. So began a very happy and profitable few days among these dear folk. The believers were encouraged, the chief and village leaders were assured of our interest and many were added to the church. I made a good recovery and we returned home rejoicing in the goodness of the Lord.

My second surgical emergency occurred one morning at 7 a.m. I was sitting at breakfast when, all round the house, people began to scream. Hurrying down the wooden stairway, I found William Usen propped up against the wall, his face a pale creamy colour and blood pumping out of his foot. He gazed at me like a man taking a last look at his friend before passing out. Losing no time we carried him upstairs and I quickly clipped the blood vessel with artery forceps.

With the foot propped up and the bleeding stopped, I covered it with a clean towel and sat down to finish my breakfast. My apparent unconcern amazed William, but helped to calm his nervous state as he thought he was dying. Before long he was able to explain how the blood vessel had been severed when he accidentally jumped on a glass tumbler. He was able to extract a piece of glass from the wound and, with help, managed to walk back home.

Because of district engagements, I had to leave William to do the daily dressings himself. On my return after some days, however, I found him in great pain with much swelling in foot and ankle. Clearly it would have to be opened up. In his own house I explored the wound under anaesthetic but could only find a small piece of glass, so the daily dressings continued.

I had to be absent again for a few days and, to my dismay, on my return poor William was in as great pain as ever. Using the last of my chloroform, I made an incision to drain pus from the swollen region. Then, having exhausted all my knowledge and resources, with his foot on a towel on my knees I prayed,

"Lord, I have done all I can. Please heal William's foot."

While I was praying he opened his eyes. Six weeks later he was on his bicycle travelling round the district with me again. After I left Mbioto for my first furlough, William continued to work with my successor, until he was called to follow the late David Ekong as pastor of the mother church at Ibeno.

These, then, were some of the memories that Pastor William and I shared, as we looked into each other's face on that thanksgiving day in October 1978. If reunion on earth can be so sweet, what will it be in the heavenly home?

CHAPTER THREE

Right Inside

When God called me to Nigeria, I little thought that one day a bonny baby girl would be introduced to me as my great-grand-child! Yet this is just what happened in October 1978. I was staying with my niece, Dr. Esther Davis at the Q.I.C. Leprosy hospital at Ekpene Obum, and from there had been taken to visit old friends at Ikot Edong. While I chatted with Mma Aggie, a former Biblewoman and outstanding Christian, her son, Pastor Robert Ukpanah, went off in his car to collect three very special people. What a thrill when they arrived! There was Alice John, looking so well and happy. Beside her stood her daughter, holding the loveliest little princess of five months, whom she reached to me saying,

"Here is your great-grand-daughter!"*

My heart was full as I looked down at the child smiling in my arms – full of memories, full of thankfulness, and full of wonder at the ways of God. To share something of these feelings I must take you back over fifty years.

It was in 1925, on returning from my first furlough, that I was posted to Ikot Edong. The Annang people who lived in that area were still regarded with fear by neighbouring tribes, but I was to spend seven very happy years among them.

With the help of the District Evangelist and two

*Shown in cover photograph.

godly men who were later ordained as elders, I began to contact the churches, schools, preachers, and teachers. As I learned more about the way of life of the people, one custom which appalled me was the giving of brides to the highest bidder. Young men, dependant for a living on their small farms, could rarely afford the required price, so girls were usually married off to old men who already had many wives working to enrich them. A wife was really an investment, and girls were often betrothed as soon as they were born.

Wherever I went I blazed out against this horrible practice and soon was being denounced by the older folks as a disturber of their customs and hailed by the young ones as their deliverer! I wanted neither designation but gave what guidance and help was possible in the circumstances.

If the parents attended church there was some hope of persuading them to repay the young bride price, although often the money had been spent already. If the girl wanted to marry someone else, I called the young man in and asked how much money he could raise. Then the parents were pleaded with, for the sake of their daughter's happiness, to accept his offer. I knew well that the girl was so eager to begin life with someone of her own age that after marriage she would work hard to help him pay off the balance.

It was harder to reason with pagan parents, but with the girl, her hoped-for husband and church leaders all praying and pleading, and with a promise that any unpaid debt would be noted on the back of the marriage certificate, many were eventually convinced. God so helped in these matters that before long we were holding a sort of court at 8 a.m. every Monday morning, to which not only church people but pagans began to bring their troubles. It was a joy to see these young couples setting up their homes together, though at times their gratitude could be embarrassing. One of the group of girls would rush out, and, before I knew what was happening, her arms would be around my neck as she poured out her thanks amid the laughter of her friends!

Perhaps I was more sensitive to the plight of these young folk because of my own situation. Many romances had flourished at B.T.I. in Glasgow, and fellow-students had tried hard to make a match for me. Like any other young man I felt how lovely it would be to have a like-minded partner, but having already seen some tragedies, I was afraid of making any mistake which could ruin my usefulness to God. Knowing that the Mission staff was very limited and a normal furlough too short a time to form a life-partnership, I was faced with the very real possibility of permanent bachelorhood. Would I be willing for that sacrifice? There could be only one response – "Lord, if you want me to walk alone, here I am."

Before leaving me alone at Mbioto, my senior missionary had taken me by cycle and canoe to one of the remote districts which would be under my supervision. There we visited two lady missionaries who were doing outstanding work among the women and girls of Okat. Meg Semple, the taller of the two, was a quiet Ulsterwoman of great strength of character. Her companion was a gentle, brown-eyed girl, with a shy smile and a soft southern Irish brogue. Both were totally committed to the Lord and ideally suited to their task. Even now I almost hesitate to write it, but as we sat there, making general conversation, the voice of God spoke once again with unmistakable clarity to tell me that Hilda Davis would one day be my wife.

For five long years I watched the loving service of those two ladies at Okat, fearing to spoil it by declaring my own hopes. Fellow-missionaries who teased me about still being single, little realised the pain they caused, for no one but God knew what was going on in my heart as I awaited his time.

I was on my second furlough when news reached me that Hilda was leaving Okat. Another worker was being sent there and she had been appointed matron of the Mission's first hospital at Etinan. This was the moment for which I had been waiting. If Hilda was moving anywhere it might as well be to Ikot Edong!

My first approach was by letter. Hilda was staggered. "Are you sure you are not making a mistake in such an important step in your life?" she replied, and went on to advise me to forget what I had written if I was in any doubt. Later she confided that marriage had never entered her mind, and how petrified she would have been, had she guessed my thoughts at our first meeting.

Having had so long to prayerfully consider the matter I was absolutely sure, but she must be allowed time to become equally convinced that God meant us for each other. Soon after my return I went down with a severe bout of malaria. While being nursed by fellow-missionaries I learned that Hilda was worrying about me and about her own non-committal attitude. The time seemed ripe for action! An unplanned meeting one day on the bush path between Etinan hospital and Mission house provided a rare opportunity of being alone together. I took her bicycle from her – and, there and then, the great partnership was settled.

To avoid any misunderstandings on the part of African observers, our engagement was announced immediately. The secret had been kept so well that our news, conveyed by letter to Mr. and Mrs. Bill, nearly blew the roof off Ibeno Mission house! It was a disappointment to the doctor to lose a good matron for the hospital, but I was soon forgiven. How wonderfully God had planned for us, and what precious years of joy and blessing lay ahead of us in his service!

Our wedding took place on 8th December 1927, in a little Friends' Meeting House, seven miles away from Hilda's home in Enniscorthy, Co. Wexford. Here, in the quiet Irish countryside, the ten-year-old daughter of Albert and Alice Davis had come to know her parents' God, during meetings conducted by two Faith Mission pilgrims. Here she had heard Mrs. Bill and other visiting missionaries describe the need of women and girls in West Africa. Here she had responded to the call of God which eventually led to nursing training and the Qua Iboe Mission. Here we made our vows to one another in his presence.

It was unusual for hymns to be chosen in advance for Quaker weddings but we felt we must have one which would set the standard for our new life together:

> 'Seek ye first, not earthly pleasure,
> Fading joy and failing treasure,
> But the love that knows no measure
> Seek ye first.

> 'Seek this first – Be pure and holy;
> Like the Master, meek and lowly;
> Yielded to his service wholly,
> Seek this first.

> 'Seek the coming of his kingdom;
> Seek the souls around to win them,
> Seek to Jesus Christ to bring them;
> Seek this first.

'Seek this first, his promise trying,
    It is sure – all need supplying.
Heavenly things, on him relying,
    Seek ye first.'

Early in 1928 we returned to Nigeria and took up
our work at Ikot Edong. Hilda's coming was perfectly
timed to help the girls who had not been allowed to
attend school and were often prevented from going to
church. From all over the district they came to her to
be taught reading, sewing and Scripture. The help of
older schoolboys was enlisted for reading classes and
the girls poured in, eighty every Monday and as many
more on Tuesdays, for three hours' instruction. It was
demanding work but very rewarding and in after
years we were privileged to visit many of these girls in
their happy Christian homes.

One of our greatest concerns in those early days
was the plight of twins and their mothers. Twins were
believed to bring a curse and both were killed if the
witchdoctor could not decide which had the evil
spirit. The poor mother was refused a place in the
village and forbidden to draw water at certain times,
pass through farmlands or attend markets. Something
had to be done to show the love of Christ to these
unfortunate women and their children.

"Etubom! Quick if you are to save the twins across
the river!"

When this call came one day, the missionary set off
as fast as he could and on arrival the local Christians
led him to the house where the babies were born.
There was the mother with her baby on the mat, and
the witchdoctor squatting nearby.

"Where is the other baby?"

"There is no other baby," came the reply.

Going outside he made this known and immediately

40

the cry went up,

"It is not true. There were two babies."

At once everyone went running into the surrounding bush, searching in all directions.

"Here it is!" came the shout.

Only a tiny brown hand still visible through the loose clay, showed where the infant had been hurriedly buried. That little one lived for a few weeks but never really recovered from its cruel beginning.

In the case of Alice, the appeal for help had a happier outcome. One Saturday afternoon a woman with a child of three years, both like skeletons, arrived at the open door of the Mission house. We learned that she was a mother of twins, and with her one living child she had tried to survive in the forest, cut off from all human company. Somehow she heard that the white people might help her and struggled to reach us. She collapsed at our door. We had her carried in and nursed her for many days, but exposure and hunger had done their worst. One morning the little girl complained with tears that her mother would not speak to her.

"Little one, your mother has gone to be with God," we explained. "You will remain with us."

There was no relative to care for her, so the little girl grew up in our compound and was loved by all. One day we missed her. In the afternoon the teacher from the nearby school brought her back saying,

"This child came to school today to be enrolled as a scholar. When I asked her name she said it was Adiaha Etubom, but I could not write such a name without asking you about it."

Now in that area the title "Etubom" was given to all male missionaries as a term of respect, and "Adiaha" meant "eldest daughter". The teacher wondered if I would agree for the child to use my name in this very intimate way. I looked at the little mite, anxiously waiting to hear my reply.

"Adiaha, what is your name? I asked, and knowing no other father, she piped up in her childish voice,

"Adiaha Etubom."

Smiling down at her to show my approval I assured the teacher,

"Yes, that is her name."

And so it was, until in later years she decided to call herself Alice. She eventually married a fine Christian young man who was cook for the doctor at one of our Mission hospitals. Alice and John had nine children, including twins, and their lovely little granddaughter was introduced to me that day at Ikot Edong.

Following our adoption of Alice we opened a twinnery and at times had up to seven pairs of twins in our care. Gradually the people began to see that no harm befell those who befriended these helpless victims of ignorance and superstition. Some Christian women were persuaded to nurse motherless infants and fear began to be overcome by love.

This process was greatly helped by the attitude of our elders who were growing in grace and knowledge of God. One mother whose twin babies had been put to death, was cut off from farming and marketing; with no home or means of support. She was forbidden to touch another person's clothing or cooking utensils, and could only enter anyone's house if a dog or fowl had first been sacrificed to protect its inhabitants.

Taking pity on this woman, Elder Ben invited her to work for him in his section of palm bush. The heathen people believed no fruit would grow there again, but in due season the crop proved to be better than elsewhere. Next he took her to plant yams on his

42

farm. To get at it she had to pass through many other farms and everyone foretold a terrible result, but when harvest came all had their normal yield. Before Christmas a powerful chief came to visit Ben and on leaving was given a present of two very big yams.

"Who can carry these yams?" asked the chief in amazement. "My son, where did you get them?"

"From the farm the twin woman planted for me," Ben replied.

From that time onward, twin mothers were free to go where they pleased. Surely God was at work on their behalf!

Church life in Ikot Edong was not without its problems. For some time we had been aware that something was amiss but were unable to pin-point it. Eventually we discovered that the district evangelist, on whom we were so dependant, was guilty of serious offences and must be suspended from church membership. He was extremely angry and persuaded many people to take his part, so things were very unhappy until he left the district. Years later, when restored to fellowship, he thanked me for my action, but at the time this was a most painful experience in which I came to appreciate even more the fellowship of our two faithful elders.

We were burdened about the low spiritual atmosphere and, after much prayer, decided to invite three church leaders from other districts to conduct a three-days' convention. God richly blessed his servants. Many backsliders were restored and some churches experienced new life in Christ. A year later the Holy Spirit came upon believers in several areas, including Ikot Edong. We never knew where or how the awakening began. It just seemed to happen in answer to prayer. Groups of men kept coming to tell us of someone's testimony in their church, saying,

"We have not been living as we ought. Help us to get right with God."

I can still picture them kneeling round our big bed, pouring out their hearts to God, confessing failure, and asking for forgiveness and help to be different. What rejoicing as they left in renewed fellowship with their heavenly Father! This movement spread throughout the district. Churches were filled, thousands of inquirers were enrolled for instruction, and the people took us to their hearts in a new way. As one godly man put it, 'You are not now on the verandah of our houses; you are right inside!'

As is so often the case, blessing was followed by testing, and the year 1929 proved to be a critical one for all of us in Ikot Edong district. During the dry season, lack of rain and poor sanitation combine to produce waves of disease – usually measles, chickenpox or smallpox. That year the epidemic was of the most virulent type of smallpox.

The Government had no vaccine and the plague spread rapidly till every town and village was affected. Men, women and children were dying like flies, so all other work had to stop while we did what we could to save life, relieve suffering, and try to prevent further spreading of the disease. Those affected had severe haemorrhage of the skin, which looked like raw flesh, and the odour was such that to be in close contact made one feel it was impossible to escape infection.

Dr. Charlie Ross from Etinan hospital joined us in visiting the villages. In one place it seemed as if everyone had fled but when we pushed the door of a house it opened to reveal the whole family lying on the floor, covered with the disease. Those still alive were given supplies of heart tonic and disinfectant before we had to move on to the next awful scene.

The pagan medicine men and diviners made a law that anyone dying of smallpox must not be buried, believing this would enrage the spirits who had brought this sickness as a punishment, so the dead were carried out and left unburied in the bush. When this dangerous situation was reported to the authorities, police were sent to enforce burial, but even so the stench was almost unbearable. Our African helpers would often warn us,

"Put your handkerchief to your nose until we pass this place."

Hilda was a true "Friend" in the matter of "concerns." One day when the epidemic was at its height she became burdened about the wife of an outstation teacher. After cycling ten miles under a blazing sun, she entered the teacher's house and found his young wife dying of smallpox. The sick woman opened her eyes and with ebbing strength said,

"Oh, Mma, I have been a very wicked woman."

There followed a full confession of sin which had been hidden even from her husband.

"Mma," she said, straining to look in my wife's eyes, "can Jesus forgive me?"

Regardless of her own safety, Hilda bent low to comfort her with God's promises, and with a new light on her face the girl breathed out her last words,

"Oh, thank you, Lord Jesus."

Tired but satisfied, my wife arrived back at Ikot Edong with the now familiar greeting,

"I'm so thankful I went."

The strain was undermining Hilda's health and she was in grave danger of contracting the disease, so arrangements were made for her to go home – the only time we did not travel together during our many years in Nigeria. She was very worried about leaving me in such imminent danger. As she prayed, God gave her a message of comfort and before reaching the coast she sent a messenger back with the promise – *'There shall no evil befall you, neither shall any plague come nigh thy dwelling,'* Psalm 91:9-10.

This assurance gave me the strength I needed and God wonderfully fulfilled his word. Smallpox raged everywhere, right up to the Mission compound, with death in every home. Crowds of people kept coming and going from my house, touching my personal goods and shaking my hand. To have shrunk from this would have caused offence and belittled my faith in God. Yet not one case occurred within our compound, although many, including houseboys, were living there.

These days of shared suffering were not forgotten by the people of Ikot Edong and forty-five years later, when I was about to retire from active missionary service, their farewell address revealed the depths of their appreciation:

"We recall your effort in arresting the spread of the smallpox epidemic during one of the years you worked among us . . . Your effort in helping to stamp out the killings of twin mothers and their babies is remembered most affectionately. Not only did you and Mrs. Dickson, of blessed memory, open and run a clinic for the care and resuscitation of these unfortunate victims of the then barbarous society, but also you went further to adopt one of the motherless babies as your own child, whose life today is a fitting tribute and testimony of your tender-heartedness and affection for mankind."

Can you understand now, my emotions that October day in 1978 when I held in my arms the little grand-daughter of "Adiaha Etubom"?

CHAPTER FOUR

Marching Orders

Early on Friday 10th November 1978, I set out from the Qua Iboe Church Bible college to travel the familiar road north to Igala. Some aspects were the same as on my first journey in 1931. The low-lying palm bush still opened out into hilly grassland, the sandy soil still changed to warm red laterite, and the dense population was replaced by scattered villages of round grass-roofed huts.

Otherwise the circumstances were very different. Then, there was apprehension about the unknown; now, a happy anticipation of renewed friendships. Then, there was anxiety about the condition of the road; now, we could cover the 250-mile route on a reasonable tarred surface. Then, we had to search for an overnight stopping place; now, we could arrive at our destination by 6 p.m. Then, we speedily left behind all sign of Christian witness or community development; now, we passed scores of schools and churches, thriving townships with hospitals and a big modern university. Best of all, in our car, driven by a young missionary, were two students for the ministry returning to Igala to visit their families during a break from the Q.I.C. Bible College. How did the transformation begin?

Early in 1931, two of our fellow missionaries, Jim Westgarth and John Nelson set out to explore a territory which had been brought to our notice by the C.M.S. Bishop on the Niger. This land of Igala, bounded on the north by the Benue river and on the west by the Niger, had been visited in the later 1860's by Adjai Crowther, a freed slave who was then a catechist with the Church Missionary Society. Later he became a famous Bishop, and was captured and held to ransom for £1,000. In attempting his rescue the District Officer fell victim to a poisoned arrow, and the beginnings of a church in the north-west was scattered and its building burned to the ground. Now the C.M.S., unable to extend its own commitments, had invited the Qua Iboe Mission to consider work there.

Our deputation discovered a pagan people, numbering over 250,000 who were strongly influenced by the Muslim Hausas, the only Christian witnesses being a few Brethren missionaries located in one division. They were unable to interview the Attah or King-Priest of Igala, but were given to understand that no foreigner would be granted residence in the capital town of Idah. Seventeen miles away at Gwalawo, however, the people appeared anxious to welcome them, subject to the consent of their Paramount Chief. Indeed, shortly before this, a number of young men had gone to the District Officer requesting that someone should be sent to teach them about God. Summing up their findings the missionaries reported:

"We found the two necessary factors that should determine the commencement of mission work in any country. First, the appalling need of a people in heathen darkness, and second, their desire to hear the word of God."

At the time of this survey my wife and I were on furlough, but joining in prayer for God's guidance to the area of his choice for a new church and mission outreach. Towards the end of June we arrived at Portstewart for the North of Ireland "Keswick"

Convention, looking forward to the refreshing sea breezes, the Bible ministry and the warm fellowship of the Qua Iboe Mission house-party. On the doorstep stood our General Secretary, R.L. McKeown. After welcoming us he dropped the bomb-shell,

"You'll be interested to know that you and David O'Neill have been chosen for Igala."

We were stunned. Blindly collecting our belongings we followed him to our room. Once alone, without waiting to remove coats or hats, we fell on our knees at the bedside with hearts too full for words. Could it be God's will to remove us from the work that was showing such promise at Ikot Edong? What about the little children who looked on us as their parents? How could we face a new language, people, customs and country?

It was not easy to join in the happy conversation at tea that evening with our thoughts in such turmoil. Sensing our distress, Mr. McKeown tried to reassure us that this was no man-made decision:

"If it's any comfort I can tell you that the letter from the Field Executive suggesting the appointment, crossed in the mail with one from Home Council with a similar proposal."

This knowledge helped to reconcile us, and confirmation came as we read "Daily Light" on the morning of Wednesday, 24th June – *"The ark of the covenant of the Lord went before them to search out a resting place for them . . . He shall choose our inheritance for us . . . This is the way, walk ye in it . . ."* Before the end of the convention we were ready for whatever God required – even if it meant Igala.

Three months later, after a great welcome back, we had to tell our friends at Ikot Edong that we soon must leave them. There was one bright spot, however. During furlough we had gone into the Belfast office and my wife had been handed an envelope containing an application from a missionary candidate in Scotland.

"There's your lady worker for Ikot Edong," prophesied the General Secretary.

He proved to be correct. Marie Brown was indeed God's answer to the prayers of the women who had asked my wife to bring back someone to help her and the prospect of her coming was a comfort to us all.

Soon after our return I set off for my first visit to Igala, accompanied by three other missionaries, Will Wheatley, Isaac McEwan and Jimmy Hutton. We had just managed to purchase an Austin 7 at the modest price of £135 and into this, and another of similar size, we packed ourselves and the necessary provisions, bedding and cooking utensils for our expedition.

By nightfall we had covered 150 miles and, having failed to locate the government rest house, we stopped at the first habitable building by the roadside. This shed, with grass roof and walls three feet high, turned out to the an outstation of the Roman Catholic mission which was active in that area. The African teacher gave us permission to camp there for the night.

We were looking forward to a tasty supper of cooked chicken but, alas, after the heat and shaking of the journey, the odour from the pot nearly knocked us down. The teacher was asked to dispose of it and next day cheerfully assured us that not even the bones had been wasted! Our breakfast menu was not much more successful. The tin of herrings being heated grew bigger and bigger, and before it could be rescued there was a hissing sound and out shot the melted fish! However, we managed to scrape up enough to give some flavour to our dry bread and enjoyed that with cups of tea.

By four o'clock we had reached Gwalawo, where David O'Neill was already in occupation. He was living in a house composed entirely of grass, which gave little protection from either sun or rain. On being questioned, he admitted that it had cost only three shillings! In order to have more time to discuss plans for the future, I shared this twelve-by-twenty-foot shack, while the others spent the night in a nearby rest house – one of the simple mud and grass shelters provided throughout the country for the use of government officials and other travellers.

The following day was busy, with much to see, to hear and to decide. That evening our fears about the weather-worthiness of our host's residence were confirmed when he became violently ill with malaria and suspected sunstroke. Neither of us got any sleep and it was clear that we could not leave him as planned the next morning. I had to get back for a conference so two of us left in my car, while two remained to nurse the patient and, on a nightmare journey, bring him back to convalesce at Etinan hospital.

Hilda was eagerly awaiting my return and together we discussed and prayed about all that I had discovered. I told her of the three hundred people who had gathered to greet us and their delight at the news that she and I hoped to live among them. I described their great physical and spiritual suffering, and how wonderfully our God was already preparing the way for us.

"Some years ago," I began, "a government officer found there were no schools from which he might hope to get office helpers, so he asked a friend at the coast to persuade an African teacher to come to Idah.

At the same time he compelled the king and his advisors to pay this man's salary. When the teacher arrived, a small school was built and he taught there till he had brought some boys up to his own standard. Later on this officer was transferred and the king and his old men closed the school and refused to pay the teacher. The boys were scattered but David has been able to get hold of three of them. They don't know much English but if we use simple words and speak slowly they can manage to interpret for us. One of them has been helping with translation and already they have a few hymns to use in the services. Hilda, you should have heard them trying to sing 'Yes, Jesus loves me.' "

This was not the only example of the blessed truth that *"when he putteth forth his own sheep, he goeth before them."* Perhaps the most remarkable instance concerned a small village from which, some years previously, a number of people had gone several days' journey to the town of Ekali, where an African preacher had told them about the one true God and pointed out the folly of worshipping ju-ju. On their return, one of the sub-chiefs had led his people in the destruction of their idols. Now they no longer made sacrifice, placed ju-ju on their farms or marketed on Sundays. They had a pathetic faith in a pot of water given them by the preacher at Ekali. Small cups of this were carefully dispensed for all ailments and the pot refilled with ordinary water. They had learned a hymn in Yoruba, of which the only recognisable word was "hallelujah", but they knew little or nothing of the way of salvation.

"The claims of Ikot Edong are great," I admitted, as we talked of all these things, "but having seen the need in the north I could never settle here again without being haunted by the condition of the Igala people."

It was clear that Hilda shared my growing conviction and from then on we began to prepare with singleness of heart for the new work to which God was directing us.

Immediately after my return from Gwalawo, another three-day conference for church leaders was held at Ikot Edong. Two hundred and thirty men were accommodated on the Mission compound and daily visitors brought the numbers up to four hundred. We were greatly burdened for these men who carried such responsibility, and had prayed long and earnestly about this conference. The ministry was shared by three African pastors and right from the beginning we felt the presence of the Lord.

The keynote was struck at the opening session with God's question, *"Where art thou?"* Two other speakers had similar messages and their addresses were searching and powerful. Between meetings we had private interviews, and after the last gathering twenty-five men came to the pastors to confess failures and seek advice on how to get right with God. I was busy seeing enquirers till 2 a.m. and others came on Saturday morning. It was blessed to see light in faces that had been clouded by sin and shame, as we pointed them to the promise in 1 John 1:9. What we could not have done in years, the Holy Spirit accomplished in a few hours.

By February 1932, Marie Brown had arrived, so, leaving the two ladies in charge, I returned to Igala to help David O'Neill build a more suitable house and prepare for the opening of our second mission station. One of our houseboys who was learning carpentry, accompanied me and this time the journey seemed less daunting, but an incident as we were crossing the Anambra river made us realise how much we had to learn about the different beliefs and customs of the Igalas. Hot and thirsty from the journey, my companion stooped over the edge of the pontoon to wash his hands and scoop up some water to drink.

"I afo, I afo," roared one of the Igalas, and I was just in time to prevent the poor boy being cracked over the head with a bamboo pole. There was great commotion for a while but eventually we got away and continued our journey. Evidently a canoe had once capsized there and a number of people were drowned. The catastrophe was put down to an evil spirit and from that time no one was allowed to wash or drink at that side of the river. "I afo" means "It is sacred" – and therefore forbidden.

Darkness surrounded us as we drove on through the forest. Strange animals loped across the road and the light of our headlamps was reflected from bright eyes in the undergrowth. We did not feel at all like missionary heroes and were very thankful to our heavenly Father when we reached our destination safely.

During my two months in Gwalawo I was able to do some medical work as well as help with building. One Sunday during the service the report of a gun was heard, not far away. Everyone looked at each other in alarm and fled in the direction of the sound. It was discovered that the small son of the District Head had got a box to stand on and taken down his father's gun. He tried to fire it but the weapon exploded in his face, causing bad burns. When the child was brought to me I lifted my heart for special guidance, knowing that the father had been at the service and would be told that this had happened because he was listening to the word of God. My medical supplies were very limited. What could I use without risk of damaging those little eyes with no eyelashes? Ah, here is the very thing – castor oil. This was poured gently over his face and head, and covered with an oily cloth. Day by day as I attended him the old skin came off and new skin grew. Instead of hindering the Gospel, the event actually won more confidence and prepared the way for vast dispensary contacts in coming days.

Back down at Ikot Edong again, we had some busy weeks before our final departure. Most of my time was spent with the two elders, examining about two thousand inquirers, of whom three hundred and ninety-eight were accepted for church membership. Many of these were young people who had begun to follow our Lord Jesus Christ during the times of blessing in the previous two years. They were baptised before we left, while others were referred for further instruction. How gracious of our God to give us this crowning joy among our beloved Annang friends!

But now our sights must be set on Igala. On my last visit I had left the boy to help with building work and now we were to take his wife, Sarah, to join him there. Like Hilda, it was her first journey north. The great day came and, with our few belongings, we set off in the baby Austin. By now I knew the way a little better and we reached the rest house just before dark. Supper was cooked on the Primus and camp-beds made up for the night. Sarah looked round, petrified at the thought of sleeping in this strange place.

"Etubom, usung iduhe?" she asked ("Is there no door?")

Something had to be done to allay her fears, so I moved my bed across the doorless entrance to ensure that no one could enter without disturbing me. This arrangement satisfied her, and we settled down to rest in the safe keeping of the good Shepherd, who said of himself, *"I am the Door."*

After a very early breakfast we resumed our journey. Just before the provincial boundary we came to a steep hill, the sight of which filled us with horror. Heavy rains had cut a gulley six feet deep, running down the whole way, sometimes in the middle of the road and sometimes winding to either side. The ladies were scared and decided to walk, but the driver had to stick at the wheel and do his best. Slowly, foot by foot, the little car moved till safe at the bottom.

Along the mile of valley we went till we reached the next ascent, my passengers again electing to lighten the load. Here there was greater risk, as the car had to be kept moving in order to get up the steep gradient. Half way up, a ledge of rock about three inches high stretched right across the road. To get a run at this the engine had to be accelerated. With fervent prayer and a big bump we were over, and had no other major problems for the next sixty miles to Gwalawo.

We kept David O'Neill company for about six weeks, visiting Adoru to get things ready for our transfer to that town, some fifty miles away, which had been chosen as the Mission's second centre in Igala. When all seemed in order, we arranged for two local lorries to transport all our belongings, plus a quantity of building materials, to the proposed site. Then, to our dismay, we discovered that the necessary permit had not yet been received from the Residence Office, two days' journey up-river. Should we cancel the lorries, or go ahead and trust God to open up the way? After carefully considering the difficulties of cancellation we decided on the latter course.

The laden lorries were sent off first and we

followed by car, stopping at the District Office to apply for a temporary permit. While Hilda sat praying outside, I went in and was greeted by an African clerk who rose from his typewriter with a paper in his hand.

"As you are here in person I don't need to send this to you,"he said.

I looked at the document and read, "Permission is herewith granted to Qua Iboe Mission to occupy the site in Adoru applied for." It was dated that very day, 19th July 1932 – a date we would never forget.

Our temporary home was situated on rising ground just outside Adoru. No path had yet been cut to it, so everything had to be carried through elephant grass, eight to ten feet high. When the lorries departed, I got two men to flatten out a track by walking up towards the huts, bending the grass on either side. Then they retraced their steps to point out holes and rocks and roots,while the little car crept up behind.

Our Qua Iboe helpers had already arrived and were sitting on their loads, looking as if the end of all good had come. However, soon all were busy, as we had a lot to do before dark. It was the rainy season and the ground was very damp. The sky could be seen through the grass roof so waterproofs were strung up over the mosquito nets to divert the rain from our camp beds. One of the boys helped my wife with the evening meal while the others settled into their round huts a few yards away, hidden by the all-enveloping grass. After supper I went to see how they were getting on. They still looked miserable but we got out our Efik hymn books and Bibles, and after singing and reading the twenty-third psalm and having a little talk together, everyone cheered up.

Back at our own hut, Hilda and I stood outside, viewing the wall of grass around us and listening to the queer sounds coming from it. All seemed so desolate. We were strangers in a strange land, among a strange people with customs we did not understand and a language that had yet to be mastered. 'Would there ever be any Christians here like those we had left down-country?' we wondered, as, tired and a bit apprehensive, we turned into our new abode. There was no door to shut and those weird noises kept echoing in our ears. Would we be safe for the night when animals came forth seeking their meat? Might we not seem legitimate prey? It was enough. Our two folding chairs, a basin and a bucket were piled up in the doorway. If any uninvited guest tried to enter, he would at least set off an alarm!

After all that we sat down for our evening devotions. Part of our reading was from "Daily Light" for the evening of July 19th. We had looked out on the wilderness and wondered if we would ever see fruit there. It was God's turn to speak once again:

"There the Lord commanded the blessing, even life for evermore . . . As the rain cometh down and the snow from heaven, and returneth not thither, but watereth the earth and maketh it bring forth and bud, that it may give seed to the sower, and bread to the eater: so shall my word be that goeth forth out of my mouth; it shall not return unto me void, but shall accomplish that which I please, and shall prosper in the thing whereto I send it . . . God giveth not the Spirit by measure unto him . . . And of his fulness have all we received, and grace for grace . . . It is like the precious ointment upon the head . . . even Aaron's . . . that went down to the skirts of his garments."

What a God is ours! What a message! What power! What equipping! And wonder of wonders, he allowed me to live long enough to see his promises come true!

CHAPTER FIVE

First Fruits

The members of Adoru church had hoped to see me at their morning service on Sunday 3rd December 1978, but I was preaching thirty-four miles away and only managed to reach them in time for the smaller afternoon service. Nevertheless it was rewarding to see some familiar faces in the congregation and to renew fellowship with old friends. One of these was Idachaba, the first Christian convert in that area; another was Oboni, our little houseboy ... but to tell their stories we must go away back to 20th July 1932.

First impressions are always important and we were very anxious to get onto a sound footing with our new neighbours. We didn't have to wait long for an introduction. Early on the day after our arrival, Idachaba and another local man presented themselves outside our house. Did we need help? We did, and soon set them a small job. Next to appear was the District Head, accompanied by many of his people.

"Do you require workmen?" he asked through our interpreter. "If you do I will provide them."

Experience had taught caution, so I replied that I had already employed two men. Obviously surprised, he enquired who they were and the men came forward from the crowd now swarming around us. Stooping before him till their heads touched the ground, they begged his pardon for failing to ask his permission. This was what I expected and provided the clue for my next move.

"If you give me workmen, who will pay them?"

"That depends on you," he returned with a smile.

"In that case I would need to employ them myself. But if you can recommend any good labourers I will certainly give them a trial."

I asked what should be the rate of pay.

"The Government pays labourers fourpence a day and we would expect the missionary to pay the same," he stipulated.

The bargain was agreed. Now we knew where we stood with each other and work could begin in earnest.

Our first job was to clear a path up to the huts. The next was to erect a more watertight and permanent house. But where could we get sand to mix with the cement? It transpired that the nearest supply was at a stream six miles away, four miles along the road and two more through the bush. Each morning a group of men set off for this spot where they dived underwater to bring out the sand, which was then carried to the roadside. In the evening every man brought home a load on his head and I went in the little car to collect the remainder in a tea-chest. In this way we made cement blocks for strong pillars to support a corrugated iron roof.

It was three months before this house was ready for occupation and meantime we continued to live in our "haystack". Heavy rains soon turned the site into a real mud bath so we laid planks to form a pathway from hut to hut. One night, while we were having our meal, a terrific tornado blew up. When the worst of it was over my wife ventured out to "walk the plank" to our bedroom. Hearing her call I followed, only to find the grass floor mats floating on three inches of water! We summoned help to dig a trench to carry the flood away, but it was about a week before that hut was dry.

Previous to our arrival a number of animals had their home in the vicinity. The cutting of the grass exposed most of these, but one reptile remained below the surface for some months before we got time to deal with it. Finally we unearthed a hibernating python, sixteen feet long, with over forty eggs in its nest ready for hatching. The Africans were very glad I only asked for the skin, as they all enjoyed a grand supper. Next morning I enquired what had happed to the eggs. They looked at each other and smiled,

"They made lovely soup," they said, and added hesitantly, "We hope another will come along soon."

Their hope was not shared by the missionaries!

Every morning and evening we held a short service for the labourers and the few small Igala boys who were brave enough to live on the white man's compound. They quickly picked up some of the choruses and texts translated by David O'Neill, and early on the first Sunday morning two boys set out to summon the people. Ringing a handbell they marched through the village calling out,

"This is the day the white man wants you to come to hear the word of God."

By 9 a.m. about sixty villagers were seated on grass mats, under the rough shelter erected to shield our car from the sun. Suddenly the message went round,

"The Onu is coming with his head wife"

Now the Onu was head chief of this district, third in rank under the Attah or King-Priest of Igala and the Achadu who had charge of ceremonials. We couldn't very well expect such an important personage to sit on the ground among his people, so two nice clean boxes were hastily found for our honoured guests.

How does one begin a service for people without Bibles of hymnbooks, who cannot read and have never heard the name of Jesus? Obviously every move has to be explained as we go along.

"This word of God can be sung in praise to him and I want you to repeat these words after us, 'Jisus I lekwu, tod'ebiene mi, n'afedo. Jisus, I lekwu k'oji mi.' (Jesus died because of my sin, I will love Jesus, he died in my stead.)"

When repetition was not too bad we tried the tune. At first everyone sang in his own key but soon we were doing well enough to pass on to prayer. This too had to be carefully explained. After a brief petition we repeated the chorus, and then came to the unforgettable experience of telling these people the wonderful story of God's redeeming grace in our Lord Jesus Christ. What an attentive audience, with the old chief hanging on every word – so familiar to us but so new to him! The sowing of the good seed had begun, but we were well aware that much hard work and patient prayer would be needed before the harvest could be reaped.

One of the best ways to show the love of God and prepare hearts for his word was through medical care, and news soon got around that one of our little huts had been set aside as a dispensary. Every fourth day there was a market at Adoru and before long we were having up to four hundred patients on those days. Truly they were in need of the help we could give them. Young and old were covered with yaws and other sores which responded quickly to our medicines and injections. No wonder they came in their hundreds! We would come out of our hut about 5.30 a.m. to find crowds already waiting, having travelled through the night to be in good time. Little children were carried for many miles in boxes on the heads of their parents, small curly heads bobbing above the elephant grass as they jogged along the bush paths.

Within eleven months of our arrival at Adoru, thirteen thousand patients had been treated, and when he heard of it, the government doctor, stationed 130 miles away, exclaimed with astonishment,

"Thirteen thousand who would never had been helped if you missionaries had not been here!"

You can imagine how busy we were from morning till night, with building, services, medical work, visitation in the village, preaching in the markets, meetings for women, Sunday School and the beginning of day school for which lessons had to be prepared and typed. Often when we were very tired the devil sought to discourage us, but we had God's promises and the assurance that many dear friends at home and down south were remembering us in prayer. Surely the good seed was germinating in some prepared hearts?

In spite of their initial fears, the apprentice carpenters from Qua Iboe had settled well and worked hard, making friends with the local workmen and helping to teach them to read. Before leaving for home they decided to hold a special service for these men. At its close Idachaba stood up and said,

"I want to bring my ju-jus and burn them before our friends go away."

Needless to say, the boys were delighted to postpone their departure for such a cause, and arranged to meet again the next day. A pile of dried grass was gathered and on this Idachaba laid his precious objects of worship – pieces of cloth and feathers, wooden figures and clay pots. The other Igalas watched from a distance, afraid to be too closely associated with this bold action, in case the curse of the spirits represented would come upon them. Striking a match to kindle a fire, the new believer challenged his idols.

"If you have any power, save yourselves now!"

As the flames rose he went on to confess his faith in Jesus Christ. Standing beside him I trembled and perspired, aware of the ruthless enemy whose stronghold was being invaded. Only the risen Lord could deliver from his grip – *"having spoiled principalities and powers, he made a show of them openly, triumphing over them in it."*

That evening the Qua Iboe boys conducted another meeting. One recalled the conversion of his father in the early mission days down south, a second spoke of the power of the name of Jesus in everyday life, and the third finished up with the exhortation, "Go and tell." Before the service ended, another local man exclaimed,

"I'll bring my gods and burn them tomorrow. I too want to follow Jesus."

The following Sunday he confessed his faith before a hundred people, including his father and the Onu, who by now were attending our services regularly.

The next few months tested the reality of these conversions. Idachaba and his wife had been married for nine years without children. It seemed to this poor woman that their last hope of a family had disappeared in the smoke of that bonfire, and she was very angry with her husband. They lived near us and by teaching and friendship we tried to show her something of the love of God. One happy day she came to tell us that she too wanted to follow Jesus, and what a privilege it was for Hilda to lead her to him. Some months later she had the further joy of assisting at the birth of a lovely little baby daughter, God's gift to the first Christian couple at Adoru. Not only did this little one survive without any of the usual pagan sacrifices, but two others were born in due course, bringing delight to their parents and confirming the faith of the growing group of believers.

Our first Inquirers' Class was held on 1st March 1933, when twenty-five names were enrolled. All of these gave a short explanation of why they wanted to join and in most cases this amounted to a confession of faith in Christ. Having experience of mass movements which could result in nominal Christianity, we were determined that church membership should not be made too easy, for these men and women were the first to bear the name of Christ in their area, and would set the standard for future generations.

Two years later, after careful instruction and the testing of time, fourteen men and one woman con- fessed Christ in baptism. The woman was Ochunia. She was tall and of stately bearing, but very poor. One Sunday morning she had waited after the service to ask how she could commit her life to the Lord Jesus. It was hard for Ochunia to admit her need. She had never murdered anyone or stolen anything; how then could she be a sinner?

Hilda gently explained to her what constituted sin in the eyes of God. As she spoke the dear woman bowed her head and said with quiet dignity,

"If that is sin in God's sight, I am indeed a sinner."

From that point it was only a step to the Saviour, and Ochunia never turned back from following him. I still remember the wonder and joy on her face as she was baptised, and her words to us that evening,

"I will work for Jesus till the end of my life."

For many years Ochunia kept her promise, bringing many heathen women to the class which my wife conducted in Adoru town every Sunday afternoon and passing through testing times of sickness and temptation with unshaken faith. In her last illness she called some of the Christians to her tiny home and said,

"I know I will be going soon to Jesus and I would be glad if you would take me to one of your houses. Everything around me here is so heathen."

Her request was granted. When settled in, she had another,

"Please go and bring my things from my house. You will see an iron pot and a hen. In the roof you will find a small tin box with some money in it, and there are also some pieces of cloth."

When all were beside her she made her will.

"I want you, Mary, to have this cloth for you have often helped me. God will also reward you. Then you will sell the pot and the hen and add what you get to the money in the box. Next Sunday when I am with Jesus, tell the people in the house of God that this is Ochunia's gift to his work."

Her instructions were carried out and the whole sum, which came to about eight shillings, was laid on the table in the little church as her thank-offering to God for his goodness. Where could you find a wiser woman, who invested all she had in the Kingdom before going in to see the King?

Among the first men to be baptised at Adoru were Idachaba and our houseboy Peter Deji. Peter's father had been a native of Ilorin, a Muslim with a large harem and many servants. While Peter was quite young his father died and he was brought to Igala by his mother and grandfather. Within five years they also died and so he went to live with a Yoruba farmer.   When we came to Adoru, Peter thought he would like to work for us, but was afraid he might not be accepted because of his Muslim faith. We assured him that we would not interfere with his religion but give him an opportunity to judge for himself which was the better way. Many things were strange to the lad but before long we could see that the word of God was at work in his heart.

Peter's people turned against him and for a time he was afraid to return home. He joined a group of Muslims who met in a shed each evening and found that one of them had a Hausa New Testament.

"Will you teach me to read?" he asked.

"You can learn from this book," they replied.

He opened it at John's Gospel, chapter three, and, as he learned to read, he began to explain the meaning of the words. His friends listened attentively and asked many questions which he then brought home to me. So through this boy the Good News reached minds and hearts that might otherwise have been closed to its message.

Our main contact with Muslims was at open-air meetings in Adoru market place. They loved to make sport of what they called "the white man's gospel," and many a time I thanked God for the ability to see the funny side of these encounters. One day one of them became a bit exasperated and exclaimed,

"How is it that if you put the Bible in the fire it will burn, but if the Koran is put in the fire it will be unharmed?"

Now this might seem a small matter to us, but to the Igalas it was a challenge.

"Go and bring me a copy of your Koran," I replied. "We will show the people whether it will burn or not."

Still maintaining it would not burn, he turned round to consult his friends. I could see it would do no good to disgrace him before them so I reasoned,

"Don't be foolish. If your big men know you are saying these things they will be angry with you."

However, not to be outdone, he went off asserting that he would bring the Koran next day for a public demonstration.

At the appointed time I turned up with a bag of dry shavings from the carpenter's shop, but no Muslims were to be seen. After considerable delay the man appeared and our little interpreter called out,

"What about your book?"

"Oh," he said, "it will be here at two o'clock."

No book arrived; on further enquiry he admitted,

"Our big men would not give the book because they have only one copy."

"Oh," I countered, before the expectant crowd, "couldn't you give it back to them after it had defied the fire?"

With typical African good humour a smile broke on his face and he said no more.

Having gained the point, I gently assured them that I was not annoyed, and invited him and his friends to come and hear more about the love of God. Sure enough, many of them turned up, as friendly as could be, at the next Sunday morning service.

Among the first small boys to help us in the house and attend our little school was one called Oboni. After visiting his home on one occasion he came to me with a serious look on his usually cheerful face.

"Big men very angry with me, Baba," he said, using the intimate term for father which was to become my familiar Igala name. Then he added ominously, "They are coming to see missionary."

By degrees I managed to get the story out of him. The headmen of his village had been preparing to make sacrifice. With great solemnity they gathered round a fowl which was tied to a post awaiting its fate. At a distance, Oboni was summing up the situation. He had heard the missionary say that, because Jesus had died, it was no longer necessary to sacrifice birds or beasts, and made up his mind to free the victim. Darting to the post, he cut the string and sent the hen squawking into the bush. Great was the anger of the heathen men, but, to everyone's relief, they never turned up at the Mission house.

Little Oboni was the means of bringing most of his family to hear the word of God. His mother was the first to announce in 1936,

"Whatever my husband does, I'm going to follow Jesus and have nothing more to do with sacrifice."

Her husband was a pagan diviner, but soon afterwards he and his brother joined her in building houses near ours so that they could attend all the services. Oboni's mother was a very fine character and we looked forward to her help among the local women, who were obviously impressed when her baby daughter was born safely without the performance of any heathen customs. Oboni was delighted about it all and as busy as could be with his lessons, household chores and the group of tiny tots whom he was teaching in my wife's four-class Sunday School.

Four months later the blow fell, with the sudden appearance of a severe rash on the mother's body which developed into fearful sores, requiring constant dressings. Hilda attended her day and night and she bore her suffering with great patience, but her condition continued to grow steadily worse.

One day I raised the all-important question,

"What if you should die?"

"I will go to the place of Jesus," she replied without hesitation.

"But can we go there with our sin?" I pursued, anxious to be sure she understood.

"No," she said with quiet assurance, "but the blood of Jesus has taken my sin all away."

Realising that we could do no more for her, we took her to a small C.M.S. hospital at Nsukka, hoping and praying for some relief. Six days later, news of her death followed us back to Adoru.

Amid great grief we packed as many relatives as possible into the car and set off for Nsukka where the funeral was to take place. At the hospital, little Oboni laid his head against me and sobbed out his sorrow, for he dearly loved his mother. Through his tears, he managed to interpret as I read a few portions of Scripture at the graveside. Then, as best we could, we sang, "Jesus loves me," ending with the verse, "Jesus Christ loves me – he will stand behind me – I will love him. If I die he will take me to his house."

"This is not your loved one we are lowering into the grave," I assured them. "This is only the house she has left to go to a far better one. Now she is free from all pain and with the Saviour in whom she trusted."

It was dark by the time we returned to Adoru. Oboni's father quieted those who were weeping, saying,

"Don't cry, she is with Jesus."

Poor man, he had watched over her so carefully and was really worn out. Two months later he too was dead, probably due to poisoning, which he firmly believed had been the cause of his wife's illness. What was now to become of the five children? We did not want to see them becoming unpaid servants under heathen influence, so, with the consent of the authorities, the entire family came to live on the Mission compound.

Baby Aladi grew to be a particularly affectionate and happy little girl. Every evening as we sat at our meal after the heat and rush of the day, her curly head would appear at the table. Two chubby brown arms would go up to each of us in turn for a goodnight hug and kiss, then, contented, she would trot off with a sandwich to munch on her way to bed. For seventeen years she lived with us. Some folk wondered if we would bring her back to Britain but we felt this would be unwise and were glad when eventually she was married to a Christian teacher.

Aladi was not at Adoru in 1978, but I met her and her husband afterwards at Idah. Oboni was present, however, at that Sunday afternoon service, accompanied by his wife. He is a trained teacher and active in the church, passing on to his family and pupils the lessons first learned in our little school. And Idachaba was there, restored after a lapse of some years and now, with his wife, a respected church leader.

Truly our God had kept the promises given to us that first night at Adoru over forty-seven years ago!

CHAPTER SIX

On Trek

One of the lasting impressions from my latest visit has been of the amazing opportunities in schools and colleges. Religious education is compulsory in all secondary schools, and except for Muslims who use the Koran, every pupil must have a copy of the Bible in the Revised Standard Version. Owing to an acute shortage of trained nationals, missionaries are warmly welcomed to teach Bible Knowledge in a great number of government and community schools which are springing up all over the country.

At 8 a.m. one Monday morning in November 1978, I stood on the verandah of a classroom at Alloma Teachers' Training College. Beside me were the Nigerian staff and the local Qua Iboe missionary, Graham Trice, who, in addition to his church work, spends a day each week teaching Scripture there. In front of us a thousand young people of both sexes were lined up for their morning assembly, eager to hear from someone who had known this area long before they were born.

An amused and excited stir greeted my efforts to address them in their own language, though English is now the accepted medium of education. I recalled my first visit to Alloma, the clinic and service we held in the town centre, and the request of the District Head for a teacher to be located there. Then, with my heart going out to these lovely young folk, I spoke about God's good plan for their lives, urging them to accept Jesus as Saviour and commit themselves fully to him.

What a contrast between the scene that day and the one which greeted my arrival after trekking about 30 miles over the hills from Adoru in the early 1930's! By then our work in the dispensary was becoming known far and wide, sometimes with surprising results. Distant stations of the Church Missionary Society had noticed newcomers at their services and, on enquiring the reason, one African pastor was told,

"We heard the word of God at Adoru dispensary and the white man told us to attend church if there was one in our home town that taught the Bible."

Later this pastor visited us and reported that a new church had to be built to accommodate his growing congregation. Most of our patients, however, were from villages where the Gospel was unknown and we had many invitations to visit these places. The whole country lay open before us, so, as soon as it seemed possible to leave my wife to supervise the work at Adoru, I recruited about ten carriers and set off for the interior with camping equipment and stocks of medicine.

The going was rough, across streams and along bush paths, broken and stony, with many detours. When a tree fell, people just walked round it, adding a new bit to the journey until it rotted and became suitable for firewood, when it would be chopped away. A bicycle was useful when there was a stretch fit to ride on, but at other times the rider had to carry the machine! Indeed there were places where progress could only be made by wading chest-deep through muddy flood water.

Most days we managed to cover eight to ten miles, usually trying to reach a village before the intense heat of noon. After a meal and a short rest we began visitation. At each compound or house we would explain our reason for coming, invite people to an evening meeting, attend to any urgent cases of illness and tell the others when to come for treatment. Of course the chief was the first to be visited and he would select the meeting place and send the town-crier with his gong to call the people. Soon the whole town would be gathered together to see the lantern slides and hear the name and story of Jesus for the very first time.

On these cross-country treks we sometimes found clear evidence that the Holy Spirit had been preparing hearts for our coming. There was the old man who, in the course of his travels, had found a member of the Nupe tribe with a book of Bible stories which he could read in his own language. So enthralling were these tales that the old man persuaded the Nupe to come and live with him, promising food and shelter in return for teaching from this wonderful book.

What a thrill to talk with these two! They knew nothing of repentance toward God and faith in Jesus Christ but were eager to be taught. Before leaving, the old man asked me to take one of his children to live with us and learn more of this message. So the small boy came to Adoru, attended our little school and became one of our first Igala evangelists.

Our travels also brought us face to face with paganism in the raw. In one place a woman with long hair, unwashed or dressed for months, was on her way to an idol before which she had promised a large offering if she was given a child. After the birth of this child she found herself unable to pay and was going to beg for time, or to be kept as a slave until someone redeemed her. So great was the fear of these idols that those under their power would choose slavery rather than risk remaining at home with an unfulfilled vow and a curse hanging over them.

In other areas people were wandering homeless, cast out because they had been pronounced guilty of witchcraft. Sickness, death, famine or any calamity was attributed to evil spirits and a diviner was employed to "smell out" the human medium. His decision could not be questioned and the hapless victim, whether man, woman or child, would be condemned to lifelong misery or early death.

On my first nine-day tour from Adoru I had an unforgettable introduction to the fearful results of these practices. We were preparing to leave a certain village when a father brought his son of about nine years old to get "eye medicine". I was shocked to see the terrible condition of the child's eyes and asked how it had come about. At first the father was afraid to tell the truth lest he be driven away, but my carriers were able to reassure him on that score.

The story was that the boy had been accused of witchcraft but had protested his innocence. After further trouble he was accused again, and again managed to get free. On the third occasion, however, there were only two alternatives – to take the usual penalty of being cast out, or to accept trial by ordeal. The family chose the latter, and the lad was brought to a famous shrine about eight miles from Adoru. Tied hand and foot, he was laid before the idol. Then the priest poured liquid from a gourd over the child's face as he took an awful oath, saying,

"If you are guilty of witchcraft, let this medicine destroy your eyes."

These wily men knew what potions to concoct to maintain their power over the people and, as a result, this innocent child was left with one eye destroyed and the other badly damaged. We could not blame the poor parents, whose ancient beliefs compelled them to accept that their boy was a danger to the whole community. But we did what we could to relieve suffering and show the love of him who went about doing good and healing all who were oppressed of the devil. In later days many of these unfortunate people were cared for on our mission compound, and some became fine Christians.

One of them was a little boy called Obi. My meeting with him was the sort of event that makes one conscious of God's perfect timing and leading in everyday life. I had gone into the government office on business and found the two officers already engaged with a boy of about eleven years of age. He stood before them, answering questions through an interpreter and quite unaware of my presence. This is what I overheard.

"When you were here last time you admitted that you practised witchcraft. Now you say that you do not. How do you explain this?"

"That is true, sir," replied the little fellow, "but when you arranged for me to live at the Mission I learned about Jesus Christ who is stronger than witchcraft. The Christian boys there taught me how this Jesus could come into my heart and save me. I asked him to do this and now I do not practise witchcraft any more."

The white officers looked at each other, at a loss for words.

Then one of them glanced to where I sat listening quietly.

"Mr. Dickson," he said, "can you help us about this boy?"

Now I had never seen Obi before, although I knew his story. Our compound was full to overflowing, but how could I refuse to take a boy who had just spoken so bravely for his Lord?

"He can come and live with me," I said.

The officials were obviously relieved and, when my words were interpreted, Obi came over to me, dropped to his knees, and bowed his head and said,

"Oh, thank you, sir. Let God bless you."

Obi's trouble had started two years previously with a very vivid dream. In it he thought he was in a forest where a circle of people were discussing those whom they would kill in different ways. To his great alarm they mentioned the name of an aunt with whom he was staying at that time. He pleaded so earnestly that the company agreed to leave her out of the number and for this he thanked them. Now Obi had been taught that when a person dreams, his spirit leaves his body and goes to take part in a real event. He also believed that people who do this kind of planning and killing are involved with witchcraft. So when the lad awoke he was convinced that he had been away in the night with the witchcraft people and must be one of them. Had he kept the dream to himself no harm might have been done but he burst out,

"Auntie, I dreamed about you last night and I had a great struggle to save your life."

When his aunt heard the details she became hysterical and began to scream, until all her neighbours ran to know what had happened. When the story was repeated they too were horrified and looked at Obi in great fear. How could they get rid of this threat to their safety? If they killed the boy themselves the authorities would take steps to bring the murderer to justice. The next best thing would be to take him to the Government Officer and get him sent as far away as possible.

After trying unsuccessfully to explode the idea of witchcraft, the officer realised that the boy's life was at risk and decided to send him to a missionary seventeen miles away. Here it was that Obi met the

Saviour and was set free to follow him. Two years had passed and the missionary, due to leave for furlough, had sent the lad back to report to the authorities on the very day I had business in their office.

Obi lived with us for over two years. When other boys went home for school holidays we kept him on our compound, still fearing for his safety. When he was about thirteen years old he begged me to let him visit his village, some twenty miles away, to tell his own people what Jesus had done for him. I tried to dissuade him, but he still persisted.

"My people are all in darkness. I can tell them about Jesus and I'm not afraid to die."

He went and we never saw him again. When the new term began without any word of him I sent an African to make enquiries. He returned saying,

"During the holiday, after telling his people all about himself, Obi suddenly became ill and died."

"Do you think it was a natural illness?" I asked.

"No, Baba, we know how these things are done and are quite sure he was poisoned."

We were heartbroken about this lovely little fellow and realised afresh the significance of the spiritual warfare in which we were becoming more deeply involved with every passing year.

Wherever we went, people were responding to the message of the Gospel and asking for teachers to be located in their towns. Other influences were active in the land, and we were painfully aware that if we did not get in quickly with the word of truth, the vacuum would be filled with error. Appeals for more missionaries had so far been fruitless, so how could the need be met? There was only one way – by speeding up the training and placement of African evangelists.

God was continuing to call young men from Qua

Iboe, sometimes through vivid dreams and sometimes through the reports of those already working in Igala. Obedience meant real sacrifice to these men, some of whom had been educated in Etinan Boys' Institute, with prospects of well-paid jobs among their own people. Coming north meant learning a new language, getting used to strange customs and living on a very small allowance, yet by 1935 there were twelve Qua Iboe families scattered over our northern field.

Like any other missionary, these evangelists had to learn humility if they were to serve acceptably, and it was up to us to try and set a good example. If the white man shouldered his own bicycle when they came to a stream, how could the Qua Iboe boy expect an Igala to carry his for him? If the white woman cheerfully put up with unpalatable food and cramped quarters, how could a strong young African complain? If she welcomed the diseased and outcast, how could he despise them? It wasn't easy to live under such close scrutiny but it was essential if our Lord was to be represented aright.

One of the first evangelists was Fettis, an apprentice carpenter who had come up to assist in building our house. By the time that work was finished he had become so burdened by the spiritual need that he decided to stay, and was located in a village about twenty miles away from us. He had a splendid grasp of the Igala language and was soon overwhelmed by invitations to preach in various places, where he saw the public burning of many idols as people turned to God. After only three months he wrote to us:

"I know very well that it is nothing in me that is causing this blessing. I am only a sinful person but God is doing his own work."

His wife, who had been trained by Hilda at Ikot Edong, came up to join him and after staying with us for a short time they went to their own town, two days' walk over a rough, stony road.

"My body was too tired and my feet too sore," admitted the brave young wife, "but I did not trouble because we are bringing God's word to these people."

Another couple when opening a new area tackled no fewer than three new languages in the course of several years. They had difficulty in securing a site for their house and had to be satisfied with one some miles away from water. These hardships were willingly accepted, but soon a greater test overtook them. One day the Egbos returned to find that their little grass house and all their worldly possessions had been burned to the ground. Yet there, among the smouldering ashes, they resolved that nothing would turn them from the path to which God had called them. Soon afterwards the husband wrote to tell of the spread of the Gospel to no fewer than nineteen villages and of his plans for instructing the new converts.

"Please pray that the Lord will make me like good ground," he requested, "not producing sixty-fold but an hundred-fold harvest to his glory; that he will fill my heart with love, my hands with service and my soul with contentment."

Fred Egbo is now with the Lord, but his widow, back in Qua Iboe, is still serving God in the nursery school in Uyo.

Shortly after returning from furlough in 1935 my wife and I went on a ten-day trek to visit these twelve Qua Iboe families, and were greatly encouraged to see everywhere the evidence of their faithfulness. At the end of July that year, ten of them came to Adoru for a time of fellowship and teaching, which proved so helpful that we were urged to repeat the event as often as possible. Even these Qua Iboe evangelists were not enough to meet the requests, so sometimes, when asked for a teacher, I would reply,

"We have no one to spare, but if you send one or two suitable boys to Adoru we will give them training and then they can return to teach your children."

From all over the country they came, and by 1935 our little training class had provided Igala teachers for a further nine villages. So the pattern was emerging – a central station where the missionaries could welcome and prepare evangelists from the older Qua Iboe field; outstations manned by these men with their wives and families; a wider circle of villages occupied by Igala preacher-teachers, with enough training and ability to conduct simple services and teach young and old to read the word of God for themselves.

All through our missionary lives we depended greatly on the prayers of our faithful friends in the homeland and, however pressed for time, we tried to keep them informed of our progress and needs. One such letter gives some idea of the situation as it affected Alloma in October 1936.

"The work in Igala is opening up so quickly that we cannot keep pace with it. The African families who came up from Qua Iboe lately are now all settled in outstations. While here with us they helped in many ways and at the same time worked at the language till the end of August when one family was located at a big town called Alloma. This is the centre of a large district and great opportunities await to be bought up, but the workers are few. Two of our Igala evangelists are in towns quite near and these spend a week each month at Alloma to receive further help from the Qua Iboe teacher."

Effiong Udo Ema, the Qua Iboe teacher referred to in this letter, had been transferred to Alloma after starting our first little school at Adoru. He was joined there by his wife, Martha, who had been brought to us at Ikot Edong by her father when she was about seven years old. The motherless child, loved and trained by my wife and Marie Brown, became in turn a true Christian missionary, serving alongside her husband in Igala and later as a Biblewoman at Etinan Hospital. What a welcome this pair gave me in their present home at Etinan in October 1978, and how thrilled they would have been to accompany me to Alloma, to see a flourishing church and a thousand young trainee teachers in the place where God used them to help establish the very first school!

CHAPTER SEVEN

Opening Doors

It is a moving experience at any time to worship in a living fellowship of God's people. To do so in Africa is even more thrilling, and to be the focus of over a thousand Igala faces beaming their welcome to an old friend – well, as we Scots say, that's "better felt than telt!"

Returning to Idah was like coming home, for that was where Hilda and I spent our final fifteen years together in Nigeria. Earlier on the morning of Sunday, 3rd December 1978, I had addressed four hundred people at the English-speaking service. Now the big church was packed to capacity and my message was being interpreted into Igala by my friend and fellow-worker, Pastor Joseph Okpanachi. As I listened to his fluent speech, I recalled the days when he pedalled far and wide along dusty tracks to take the Gospel to surrounding villages, always carrying a dictionary and often consulting it to improve his vocabulary of English words. As a result of this diligence he became a skilled interpreter, and later assisted me greatly in the revision of the Igala New Testament.

Joseph was involved from the very beginning of the church at Idah. He was one of a class of boys who met in an empty house each Sunday, to be taught by the missionary from Gwalawo. Then when my wife and I began coming once a month from Adoru he would gather with others to hear the word of God at the waterside market place.

I can still recall that scene so vividly. We met at a crossroads under the shade of a big "Flame of the Forest" tree, in season ablaze with scarlet blossom. Hilda would sit on a large stone at its foot while I stood with my little interpreter, Egbunu, encouraging him to speak clearly enough for passers-by to take notice. A hundred yards to my right stretched the broad Niger river. A similar distance to the left stood a remarkable statue, marking the burial place of an Igala princess.

Idah was the capital town of Igala, where the Attah 'Gala, or King-Priest, had his residence. We had heard about this ruler and his proud predecessors, one of whom was famous for having rejected the personal gifts of Queen Victoria as unworthy of acceptance, when he received the Niger Expedition in 1841. Attah 'Gala was regarded as semi-divine and forbidden to touch the bare earth or travel on water, in case the sacred spirit should be transmitted from his body. He must not eat or drink or show any emotion in public and, in his priestly capacity, he alone could make sacrifice for the whole people.

Some two hundred years previously the Igalas had come under attack from their enemies, and it was decreed that only the sacrifice of their ruler's favourite daughter could prevent their destruction. Of her own free-will, Princess Inikpi consented to be buried alive in order to save her tribe. There, within sight of the effigy that marks that historic spot, we spoke to the people of Idah about the Son of God who loved them and gave himself for them. How would they react to that gift?

Reactions varied. Some of the Muslim listeners felt their faith threatened by the truth we taught and, years later, I was told how they had planned to stone me, but were unwilling to do it in broad daylight.

Each Sunday they waited for nightfall to bring their opportunity but, in the goodness of God, we always left before dark. In spite of this undercurrent of opposition some people were showing interest, notably three elderly women who later formed the nucleus of my wife's women's class. One of these was Joseph Okpanachi's mother.

After some training at Gwalawo, Joseph showed such promise that he was sent for further schooling in another area. He came back just in time to be appointed District Evangelist when we moved to Idah in 1938, and from then on we worked in the closest co-operation and fellowship. Joseph later studied at our Qua Iboe Church Bible College at Abak and was the first pastor to be ordained in Igala.

But how did we come to work in Idah? From their earliest survey, the Mission had realised the importance of this capital town, but, having been told that no foreigner would be permitted to live there, we contented ourselves with visiting it when possible, quietly waiting for God's time. Often, as we passed along the tree-shaded avenue we would look through the entrance to the sun-baked palace and pray for access to the Attah 'Gala who lived there with his many wives and children. Our prayer was answered in an unexpected way.

One day David O'Neill and his trainees at Gwalawo heard the trumpet blasts which heralded the approach of the paramount chief and rushed out to get a glimpse of the royal car. At the foot of the hill on which the Mission house was situated, the engine slowed down, spluttered and stopped. The driver got out to examine it and was soon joined by the missionary.

"Would the Attah 'Gala like to wait in the shade and privacy of the Mission house till the fault is repaired?" he enquired.

The offer was graciously accepted and at the end of a brief stay the host remarked casually,

"Now you have seen my house, but I have not seen yours."

What could the departing guest do but invite Mr. O'Neill and his fellow-missionaries to return the call at the palace?

In due course this gesture was confirmed by an official invitation, sealed with the Royal Elephant stamp, and the following Sunday afternoon found us in the middle of a big concourse of people before the Council Chamber. A large chair was brought out and covered with rich cloth. Presently the king himself appeared, clothed in robes of state. On his feet were slippers adorned with ostrich feathers and round his neck he wore garlands of enormous coral beads. After shaking hands, he seated himself with great dignity and granted permission to explain our reason for coming to his country. As we spoke he listened half-heartedly, while his attendants tactfully waved large fans across his face to disguise his yawns of boredom. When we finished he remarked in the customary way,

"I ch'enyo" – "It is good," and expressed his interest in our medical work at Adoru.

"Why do you not come to the sick people in my house with your medicine?" he enquired.

"I thought the king with all his medicine men and diviners would not want the white man's medicine," was our reply.

At that he laughed and proceeded to arrange for us to come once a month to treat any ailing members of his household.

As we talked, Hilda had been watching the two hundred women ranged along one side at a respectful distance from their royal husband.

"Ask the Attah if I may come sometime to talk to his wives," she told our interpreter.

"Certainly, come anytime," he readily agreed, surprised that the white woman should be interested in them.

So began our regular contacts with the royal household. Sometimes we would arrive to be told that the Attah was asleep. Few people had the right to disturb him so we waited for an hour or more till he awoke and gave the necessary permission. After attending to the sick, Hilda spoke to the women. At first they were very noisy, bursting into gales of laughter at the thought of closing their eyes for prayer. But gradually they grew more reverent, three older ladies showing particular interest which later deepened into faith.

While my wife was with the women I had opportunities to talk to the men. My interpreter, Egbono, belonged to Idah, being one of the boys who had learned English there before our arrival. When home on holiday he gathered his own people to hear the word of God, and arrived back to tell us that his mother had burned her ju-ju. All these factors prompted Hilda to put on record,

"We are very burdened about the people in Idah. It is a very big town and there is a harvest waiting for a resident worker."

Soon after this, we had a visit from two leaders of the Qua Iboe Church in our southern field, Pastor Joseph Ekandem, and Mr. Samuel Ekaluo, a teacher from Etinan. They were delighted to see the progress being made, especially in the centres manned by their own Qua Iboe evangelists. The highlight of their programme was an interview with the Attah 'Gala, when they presented the claims of Christ most graciously, witnessing to his power in their own lives. After an hour's conversation, they addressed a huge crowd in the town and were approached by a group of young men with an earnest plea that the Mission would send them a teacher without delay. The door to Idah was wide open at last!

The first missionary to live in Idah was Hugh Crockard, and we took over when he went on furlough in 1938. By then there was a small church with eleven communicant members, a little school with two Qua Iboe teachers, and a Mission house nearby. Idah was situated on a sandstone cliff leading down to the river. There were few trees for shade and the tropical sun beat pitilessly on the parched earth. Our house had been built by an inexperienced builder, and its windows were too high and small to make the most of any available air current. It was like living in an oven!

One breathless evening, annoyed by unnecessary discomfort, we were once again discussing the ventilation problem. Suddenly Hilda broke off.

"Do you know," she said. "I believe we are more concerned about those windows than we are about the salvation of the souls around us. It's not right."

I could only agree. Then and there, we vowed that the windows should never again be mentioned. And they never were.

The incident was typical of Hilda. To her, people always mattered more than things, and everyone else's needs came before her own. Up to forty patients might be treated at her morning dispensary but emergencies arrived and were dealt with at all hours of day and night. Often I would be roused from sleep by an urgent enquiry,

"Do you hear anything?"

"No," I would reply, "but we'll listen."

Sure enough the faint cry of a baby, or some other indication of need, would set us in motion – she to attend to the patient and I to supply the necessary hot water from a temperamental primus stove.

One of our chief concerns was the very high rate of infant mortality. Wherever we went we met mothers who had lost many babies within a few weeks of birth and, in a country where childlessness was socially unforgivable, their plight was pitiable indeed. If only they could be taught the basic rules of hygiene and prevented from forcing the strong "Igala medicine" down the baby's throat at the first sign of sickness, many deaths could be avoided. But how could these women be convinced of the need to change their age-old customs? Only by seeing other healthy, happy families as a result of cleanliness and proper feeding.

A small maternity ward was built behind the Mission house where mothers could come before their babies were born and be sure of help in time of need. Often they stayed for weeks or months after the birth, afraid to leave in case harm came to the precious child, and, over the years, many a mother returned home with the double joy or a living child in her arms and a living Saviour in her heart. Some in turn helped others, by caring for orphan babies, or the destitute women who also found refuge on our compound.

One day Hilda and I stood looking at a tiny four-days-old motherless infant who had just been brought in.

"What are we going to do about her?"

"Well, you know what we decided the other day – no more babies to keep you tied to the compound."

"But what will happen to this wee mite?"

"I'm afraid she has very little hope of survival. How can she live with no milk and only supply of dried food a hundred miles away?"

"It's easy to make a decision until you're faced with a helpless little baby with big brown eyes."

"I know. I feel awful too, but we have to draw the line somewhere."

As we talked, a familiar figure appeared on the verandah and Hilda had a sudden brainwave.

"If we allowed old Iye to come and live here she could look after this baby."

This was just what the old lady wanted. Ever since her conversion she had longed to move in, but we had discouraged the idea, feeling that her witness was needed among her Muslim relatives. Now it seemed to be both the solution to our problem and the answer to her prayers. So Iye Utinyo took up residence in the Mission compound and became a blessing to us all.

Often at bedtime when we went over to make sure all was well with the patients, we would hear the sound of an aged voice. Opening the door quietly we would see Iye on her knees at the bedside with her arm round a pagan mother, as she prayed for her sick child or sought to lead her to the Saviour. These poor women, unused to love, would almost worship her, and her gentle influence brought many of them to hear the word of God.

One whom she befriended was a tall middle-aged woman who was found sleeping in the market sheds. She had been happily married but when her husband died she was accused of witchcraft and driven from her village. Having no children of her own she was overjoyed to be entrusted with the care of an orphan baby. She had little idea of cleanliness or regular feeding and without her friend's guidance the task would have been impossible. However, what she lacked in knowledge she made up in good nature and trust, and when at last she presented herself for baptism, the church people testified with one accord,

"If ever there was a Christian it is this woman."

During Iye's time with us I became ill with a poisoned leg and was taken for treatment to a hospital three hundred miles away in Port Harcourt. She was very concerned. Coming one day to enquire, she found the room full of missionary visitors. The news was good and, oblivious to every one, she sank to her knees, pouring out her thanksgiving to the God who had become more real to her than any earthly friend. Indeed, near the end of her life, when Hilda tried to tempt her to eat some little tit-bit or brought some small gift, she would say quietly,

"Iye mi, Mother mine, I don't want anything but Jesus."

This changed attitude to death is one of the most powerful evidences of spiritual rebirth and it was sorely tested soon after we arrived at Idah. One evening as we talked on the verandah with our houseboys, we noticed signs of an approaching tornado.

"Quick, boys," I said. "Get to your house before the storm breaks."

No sooner had they disappeared than torrential rain began, accompanied by blinding lightning. There was a deafening crash and we heard cries from the boys. On reaching their house I found one of them dead, another helpless and the rest shocked and dazed.

We were stunned by this tragedy, especially Hilda whose natural fear of lightning had been overcome with great difficulty. The dead boy was a Christian. For him all was well, but how would it appear to other believers who were always being warned of the dire consequences of association with the strange new faith? We could only commit the outcome to God and trust the infant church to his protection. Soon Hilda was able to write home:

"The Christians helped us wonderfully. It is just marvellous to see the way they have taken this mysterious happening, so hard for even us to understand."

About the same time we suffered another severe loss through the death from tuberculosis of Alfred, who had been my wife's interpreter. Early in 1933, when struggling with one interpreter between us at Adoru, we were praying that God would send another. At that time it seemed most unlikely as there were no other boys around who knew English, but with our God all things are possible!

One day a young man arrived and addressed me in English. To my great surprise he said he was an Igala and had come for work. Our prayers seemed to be answered, but he continued,

"I don't want to deceive you, sir. I only want to work for four months. I've signed a contract with the government to be trained as a sanitary inspector and I want to earn a little while waiting to begin training."

We really needed someone permanent, but his open manner appealed to me. When I spoke about interpreting the word of God he replied that while at school, far up-river at Lokoja, he had become a member of the Roman Catholic church. This posed another problem. Dare we risk confusing our people who were only beginning to grasp the way of salvation by faith? As Hilda and I discussed how best to explain our doubts, God spoke to us,

"Did you not ask me for an interpreter? Are you going to send this man away because he doesn't meet with your approval?"

That decided us. We would give him a trial and watch to see what God would do. Days later, at evening prayers, I noticed Alfred drinking in every word. The subject of our talk was Acts 16 and when he heard how God delivered his servants and how the jailer was saved through believing on Jesus Christ, he burst out with joy. The other boys present looked disapprovingly at him as if he ought to behave better, but Alfred was hearing God's voice and was oblivious to their reactions. He came to me later, saying,

"I never heard the word of God like that before."

We talked together for a long time and from that day he was a changed person. After completing the pre-arranged training, Alfred was appointed back to Idah and, in spite of much opposition, played a large part in the beginnings of the church there. Even in his last illness he bore an effective testimony. One young man explained why he had begun to attend church by saying,

"I've been watching you and I see you are happier in your sickness than many people who are well... You are not afraid, and when folk come to sympathise you speak the word of God and comfort them instead. I have never seen it like this before. You must be trusting the true God and I want to know his way."

How often we thanked God that he had not allowed us to turn away the faithful helper he sent to us that day in 1933!

We had been feeling the urgent need for a more adequately trained ministry in the growing number of Igala churches and were delighted, in 1941, to see the opening of our Evangelists' Training School, under Solomon Irondi, a qualified teacher from our Boys' Institute at Etinan. On the first day we had fourteen students and the new principal addressed them on the parable of the mustard seed, stressing how small beginnings could lead to great usefulness. It was our fervent prayer that after completing Standard VI, these lads would take a nine-months' Bible course and go out to carry the saving message far and wide.

This was a strenuous year for me, as David O'Neill was no longer with us and I was struggling to continue the revision of the Igala New Testament on which he had been engaged. The Brethren missionary R.T. Dibble, who had done the first translation, was keen that it should be checked from the original Greek, so I had to brush up my scanty knowledge of that subject, feeling very ill-equipped to follow these two gifted men. With Joseph Okpanachi as my helper, I tried when possible to devote from 8 a.m. till noon to this revision, which was later tested out on a selected company of Igalas from different parts of the country. It was an immense relief when the task was finished, and a wonderful thrill to place the Testaments, beautifully printed by the British and Foreign Bible Society, in the eager hands of Igala Christians in 1948.

The number of believers at Idah was continuing to increase and accommodation was, in every sense of the word, a pressing problem! From its earliest meeting place under the big tree at the waterside, the congregation had moved into a simple shelter which afforded a little more protection from the elements and some privacy for worship. The site proved to be part of a government reservation so, through a gift of £60 from the mother church in Qua Iboe, a bigger building was erected on an approved piece of ground. Soon this also became too small, and, realising that its mud walls and grass roof were in constant need of repair, the members began saving for a more permanent meeting place. Week by week they set aside God's portion from their earnings and at harvest time brought special thank-offerings of money, farm produce or livestock. What squawking and bleating, what calculating and praising was heard on these occasions!

Funds were steadily mounting and the plans complete, when Evangelist Joseph arrived back from a fact-finding tour of twelve village churches. His report was disturbing. Many of these small congregations were unable to pay their preachers and the work of God was being hindered by lack of support. It was a direct challenge and the Christians rose to it nobly:

"What good will a fine building be if our Lord should return and the people of Igala are still without the Gospel?" they reasoned.

With one accord they agreed to devote every available penny to help their weaker brethren, and to begin to replenish their own building fund. Gifts poured in as never before, and, by 1952, Idah had a church seating six hundred people, with room for a substantial overflow on its verandah. Even that building soon proved inadequate for the growing congregation, and in 1960 I had the privilege of taking part in the opening of the present large cement-block church, with louvred windows and seating capacity for over a thousand people. Surely the Christians of Idah were proving once again that *"he which soweth bountifully shall reap also bountifully"*.

As I sat looking over a new and more prosperous generation in that lovely church in December 1978, I prayed that they might rise to the challenge as their parents had done before them. For there are still weak churches, under-paid preachers and unevangelised people in many parts of Nigeria.

CHAPTER EIGHT

Testing Times

One familiar face was missing from the congregation in Idah church that day in 1978, for Elder James Ogaji was ill and unable to be present. It was unthinkable that I should leave without seeing him, so after a nice meal in the preacher's house, I went to visit my old friend. He was not confined to bed and what a happy time I spent with him and his wife, Lydia, a lovely woman with queenly dignity and grace.

James had become interested in the Gospel in the early 1930's and by the time we came to live in Idah he had received Jesus as his Saviour and was attending Inquirers' class. We made no comment on the fact that he had two wives, leaving the Holy Spirit to do his own work. By and by he asked to be baptised and, as church members were not allowed to have more than one wife, the question of polygamy had to be discussed. Now James wanted to walk in God's way, so, making provision for the support of his second wife, he was united in Christian marriage to the first, whose name was then Egbono.

James grew steadily in knowledge of God and was among the first elders to be ordained at Idah. At that time he was a blacksmith to the Attah 'Gala, but as years went on he became a successful trader and contractor. With him the work of God always took the highest place and his wise decisions and discernment won great respect in the church and community.

One of his richest blessings was a good wife. Like Lydia of old, the Lord opened her heart to the truth of his word, and this was the name she chose at baptism. Lydia soon learned to read and became a great help to my wife in her work among the women and girls, but she had one big problem. Her widowed, heathen mother refused to listen to the Gospel. Again and again she came to Hilda in tears, begging her to visit the old lady. To do this involved a stiff climb up the cliffs by the riverside and a scramble down a steep path to the plain. Often they got there only to see a watchful figure dart out of the house to hide in the bush!

After many visits and much prayer the old woman began to attend church. For a while she came regularly, but the enemy of souls would not let her go easily and in a dream she heard her late husband warn that he would kill her if she continued to listen to the new teaching. This so terrified her that she became more opposed than ever. Poor Lydia had been full of hope and was now heart-broken, but she did not stop pleading that her mother might even yet seek God's mercy.

As so often happens, the answer to Lydia's prayers came in an unexpected way. One day she found her mother very ill and unable to look after herself.

"Mother, please let me bring you to my house and nurse you there," she begged.

To her surprise the sick woman agreed and was moved to her daughter's home a short distance from Idah church. As she lay there she could hear the sound of worship and one Sunday morning the singing was loud enough for her to make out the words,

'What can wash away my stain?
Nothing but the blood of Jesus.

What can make me whole again?
Nothing but the blood of Jesus.'

When Lydia returned from the service she was greeted with a wonderful request –

"I want to know more about Jesus who can take away my sin."

How well I remember the light in my wife's face as she came home with the good news,

"Lydia's mother has trusted the Lord!"

During the last weeks of her life the old lady was a totally different person, talking to everybody about her new-found Saviour and waiting contentedly for his call. As for Lydia, her thankfulness knew no bounds and her faith in God's power grew stronger and stronger.

Women's work was fast becoming a notable feature of Idah church. Following Hilda's example, the members of her classes visited regularly in the government hospital and often welcomed into their homes discharged patients who had been cast off by relatives. Every Sunday afternoon they divided into groups and went from compound to compound, sharing the message they had heard at the morning service. On alternate Sundays with their menfolk, they visited the local prison, and these contacts were so effective that a number of ex-prisoners later found their way to church and to the Saviour.

Occasionally the Christian women formed little bands and went out to "gossip the Gospel" in the villages round about. On these visits they were able to encourage isolated believers and invite them to attend the annual women's conference at Idah. This big event was timed to coincide with school holidays so that the dormitories could be used as sleeping quarters, and it was a busy time for all of us.

For weeks beforehand our compound would be

piled high with iron and clay pots, firewood and foodstuffs, all contributed voluntarily by the women of Idah church. Excitement grew as the guests began to arrive – some travelling by crowded lorry or canoe, others walking up to forty miles, heedless of swollen, aching feet and thinking only of the happy time they would have together.

Year by year the numbers increased, till over six hundred were attending. Mothers came with babies on their backs and small children at their sides, all made welcome at this family gathering. Many of the women had heathen or Muslim husbands with several other wives, and some had suffered sorely for their faith in Christ. Hilda and her helpers were never too busy to share their troubles or tend their ailments, and, in the meetings, church leaders dealt with problems and brought comfort and guidance from the word of God. Today, with no missionary located at Idah, this conference still continues under the wise leadership of Lydia and other mature Christian women, each with her own story of redeeming grace.

As the standard of education rose for boys we were concerned about the need for some training to equip girls to take their place as wives of teachers or evangelists. Some years previously a little girl had presented herself at our house at Adoru, asking to be "taught book." She could only speak the Ibo language and, regretfully, my wife had to refuse her request. Seeing the crestfallen face, she tried to soften the blow by adding,

"If you could learn Igala I might be able to take you in when we get back from furlough."

Imagine our surprise when the first one to greet us on our return, some months later, was this eager girl, bursting to announce,

"Iye, I can speak Igala now."

We were to move to Idah where the only available accommodation would be needed for boys. What could we do to keep faith with the child? Eventually we discovered that, in addition to Ibo and Igala, she could also speak a little English, so we asked her,

"Oleo, would you be willing to go a long journey to a school where all the lessons would be in English? None of the other girls would be able to speak your language. They would have different customs and eat different food. You might be very lonely away from your own people but we have no other schooling to offer at present."

Without hesitation the answer came back,

"I will go."

Before long Oleo was on her way three hundred miles south to the Grace Bill School for girls at Eket. She made such good progress there that within three years the principal was able to report to us,

"I do thank God for the work of grace in her life. She has developed good general knowledge, sound commonsense and a good bearing. Above all she is saved and growing in knowledge of God's word."

After spending a further year in G.B. School as pupil teacher, Oleo, who by now had taken the Christian name of Esther, joined us at Idah. It seemed that she, like her Old Testament namesake, had been raised up of God to meet the need of that particular time. For years my wife had been praying for a single lady missionary to develop girls' work in Igala and it was Esther's dearest wish to be prepared to help this teacher when she came. Now she was ready. But where was her fellow-worker?

Hilda's hands were too full to take on further responsibility and our compound was still an unsuitable place for permanent accommodation, but, pending a better arrangement, she had allowed seven girls to live in a dormitory near our house while they attended Idah school. Esther came to help her look after these girls and give them extra classes in Scripture and domestic subjects. Their efforts produced worthwhile results. But what might not have been accomplished for the kingdom of God if some young teacher in Britain or elsewhere had responded to the call at that time of great opportunity?

After some years Esther was married and moved to another area. Her place was taken by one of the seven, who had been redeemed from slavery to an idol by a family relative who was a leading elder in Idah church. She became a very bright Christian, as did a number of other girls who lived for longer or shorter periods in that little dormitory. It was my great joy to meet several of them with their husbands and families during my recent visit.

I cannot think of that group of girls, without recalling a very dramatic experience. One of the girls, who had recently been married, was persuaded by her mother to take an oath before an idol, in order to clear her name from some accusation. She swore a lie and within a month became mentally deranged. In those days there were no institutions for the treatment of mental illness and, to restrain her violence, her relatives had tied her hands and placed her feet in stocks. To save this girl from becoming a public spectacle we agreed to keep her in a house on our compound, trying to do what we could for her welfare.

It was a distressing situation and for many troubled weeks we wrestled with feelings of spiritual impotence and defeat. Crisis point was reached one morning in that little house where the powers of darkness seemed so strong. The girl was very agitated, throwing herself about and looking around with terror-filled eyes for the spirits that were tormenting her. Surely it could not be the Lord's will to leave her in that pitiable condition. Did I not preach about his power to cast out demons? Was he not still able to deliver? With an upsurge of faith, my heart responded –

"Lord, I believe. Let your power be made known today!"

Calling the girl by name, I talked to her about the Lord Jesus.

"You know that you trusted Jesus as your Saviour and you belong to him. He redeemed you, but when you were in trouble you swore a lie before God and before that pagan ju-ju. In doing that you opened up your whole being to the devil. He took possession and holds you in his power, but Jesus is able to deliver you. In his name, as his servant, I'm going to cast out this evil spirit."

Then, standing beside her, I said, quite simply and quietly,

"Devil or demon, whatever you are, in the name of the Lord Jesus Christ the Son of God, I command you to come out of this girl and never enter her again."

Nothing spectacular occurred, but I went and told Hilda that I was going to set the prisoner free. The cords were cut, the stocks were removed and the girl was left alone with her Lord. A short time later she walked into our house and spoke to my wife.

"Iye," she said, "I'm going home."

She was dirty and dishevelled from rolling about on the ground, so Hilda took her into the bathroom, washed her and gave her clean clothes. Then off she went to her own home. Presently the neighbours came running in fear, to tell us she had escaped.

"Leave her alone," I counselled. "Just treat her normally and see what will happen."

Sure enough, next morning the girl was up early and sweeping round her house like all the other women. She never looked back after that, and later confessed the whole matter at a women's meeting, telling how God had restored her and asking for the prayers of her friends. Eventually she entered government service as a prison wardress, and remained true and faithful for many years until the Lord took her home.

This experience proved to be a memorable one for Hilda and me. Having witnessed the power of the devil and the greater power of the risen Lord, could anyone ever be the same again? And indeed our heavenly Father knew that we would need this strengthening of faith for the years that lay ahead.

When the second world war was entering its fourth year we came home for a much needed furlough and May 1944 found us once again on the steamer bound for West Africa. Having voyaged safely through seas that were still infested with torpedoes, we landed at Lagos and decided to complete our journey as economically as possible by lorry, train and canoe – a route not to be recommended to the fainthearted!

We left at 8 a.m. on the Wednesday morning and twelve hours later were deposited with our belongings in the middle of the railway track at Oshogbo. Another train had already pulled up at the only platform and, as we groped our way through a big crowd in the darkness, the northern train also arrived, hemming us in on both sides. Somehow we managed to get off the track and find a lorry to carry our heavy loads which, after a long wait, were claimed from the goods van. How thankful we were to reach the C.M.S. Rest House at 10.30 p.m.!

After a day's rest we set out by lorry on another eleven-hour journey to the C.M.S. at Ekari, and the following morning continued to Lokoja on the river Niger. It was the dry season when the movements of river steamers are uncertain, so we decided to hire a canoe. As we travelled, the wind increased and storm clouds gathered. By 4 p.m., with a ten-hour journey still ahead of us, we were forced to seek shelter for the night at the riverside town of Etobe. No sooner had we landed than the tropical rainstorm burst upon us. Dripping wet and weary, we wondered where to turn for help. Imagine our delight then to be greeted by Effiong and Martha Udo Ema who, unknown to us, had been transferred there from Alloma. What exclamations and thanksgivings, and what happy fellowship in that little home with one of our dear "daughters" and her husband! Surely our heavenly Father always knows when his children need a special token of his loving care.

Next morning the African agent of a trading company kindly brought us down-river in his powerful launch, arriving at Idah about noon. As we approached the beach we saw several familiar figures and heard excited whoops and yells. Our former house-boys were on the look-out and soon we were surrounded by a great welcoming crowd. For days the people kept coming to greet us and to praise God for our restored health and safe return. It was almost overwhelming, but very heart-warming!

Unlike the first world war, the end of the conflict brought no flow of volunteers for missionary service and by 1945 we found ourselves in charge of all five stations in Igala and Bassa. Facing this impossible task, we could not help thinking of the crowds of young people we had seen thronging convention services and missionary meetings in the homeland.

Surely the Lord of the harvest meant some of them to be where the grain was ripe and the reapers few?

Imagine, then, with what thankfulness we welcomed a fine young English couple, who stayed with us for two months before being located in our old station at Adoru. How we enjoyed their company, and what high hopes we had for their usefulness in the coming days!

I had been having trouble with my eyes and it was decided that the cataract should be removed in 1946. We were in Belfast awaiting the operation when a cable was received from the field with the shattering news, "Eileen Broughton called home suddenly, thirteenth, phlebitis."

A few days later we received a letter from this dear girl, telling us that she would be remembering us specially on the 20th August, when my operation was due to take place, and quoting Psalm 37:39, *"The salvation of the righteous is of the Lord; He is their strength in the time of trouble."*

Reaching us as it did, after her death, this promise came like a message straight from heaven, and helped to steady us through those difficult days. It was impossible to find any human reason in the loss of such a useful life. We could only bow before an all-wise, all-loving Father and leave the explanation till that great day when all shall be made clear.

It was not only missionaries who were scarce in the mid-1940's. We had looked forward to the time when many of the boys attending Idah school would hear the call of God to become preachers and pastors to their own people. But government departments and traders were also needing educated staff and could offer attractive wages. We understood the natural desire of these young men to improve the standard of living for themselves and their families, but it was disappointing to see scores of village congregations being left without the teaching and pastoring which they so much needed.

Nevertheless, although few of the former students of that first school at Idah became preachers, many have been ordained as elders and given valuable service in various departments of church life. A number became teachers, some gaining University degrees, and among those with whom I talked on my last visit, three were past or present principals of our secondary schools at Ochaja. Thank God for such men who are exerting a Christian influence on the youth of Nigeria today – and for the privilege of giving them a helping hand.

CHAPTER NINE

The Challenge Of Bassa

Were you ever in a car which got stuck in the sand, maybe on a seaside beach on a summer's day? Well, how would you like it to happen on a lonely road by moonlight, in the heart of the Nigerian bush?

It was 6th January 1979 and David Griffiths, my missionary host, was driving me back to his home after a visit to our Kanyehu dispensary. We had spent some time with the Sisters in this busy medical centre and had a rather trying meeting with local church leaders. As we set off I thought how pleasant it would be to wash off the dry season's dust and relax for a bit before tumbling into bed. But first of all we had to face a thirty-five mile ride over a very rough road which always took its toll of car and passengers. Half way through, we hit a patch of deep sand, the wheels spun round, and we ground to a halt. Out came the spades and planks, and, after a full hour of digging, coaxing and hauling, we once again got moving. Somehow, that journey seemed to symbolise the frustrations and set-backs experienced over the years in bringing the Gospel to the Bassa people in that area of Plateau State.

Nigeria is divided into three by two great rivers which meet, roughly speaking, in the form of the letter Y. The stem and left-hand branch are formed by the Niger, and the right-hand branch is the Benue. The Qua Iboe Mission had spread upwards on the eastern side of the Niger, but, not long after our arrival in Igala, we became aware of the challenge which lay across the river Benue. It was in 1934 that two fellow-missionaries, Jim Westgarth and Eddie Dornan, and I set out to survey the Bassa country, with a view to deciding whether or not a missionary should be located there. We did not know the language and were praying that we might find someone with whom our Igala interpreter could communicate.

After a long car journey, we reached the government rest house and when our camp beds were arranged for the night we seated ourselves outside to quietly observe our surroundings. By and by, our helper, Egbunu, wandered off on his own. As my eyes followed, I saw him talking to a boy and called to ask if he had found someone from Igala. To my surprise he replied,

"No, this boy comes from Bassa Komo."

"But how are you able to talk to him?" I asked.

"Oh," he explained, "he understands Igala."

Now my mind began working. If this boy would come back with us and learn English he might become interpreter for the first missionary to the Bassas. What an exciting prospect!

"Egbunu," I said, "please call the boy that I may speak to him."

The lad seemed to be about twelve years old. He was obviously frightened by the ghostly sight of three white men but Egbunu was able to reassure him. We asked him about himself and if he would be willing to come to Igala.

"I am a Muslim," he replied. "I must ask my eldest brother if he will allow me to do this."

"Well, we leave early tomorrow morning. Please ask your brother to come and see us before we go."

Sure enough the family group turned up in good time next day and, after some discussion the brother and the local chief gave their consent, probably thinking this would be a worthwhile opportunity for the lad to rise to a good position. We had no room in our own transport so I gave Amodu enough money to travel down-river by canoe to Idah and arranged to meet him there. We returned to Adoru and on the appointed date I drove the thirty-four miles to collect him, only to find that he had already been waiting for two days – a promising sign of keenness!

Amodu soon settled in with the Igala boys on our compound, continuing to live as a Muslim but attending our morning and evening worship. This puzzled some of the Christians and one of them came to me complaining,

"That Bassa boy is hiding behind our house, praying like Muslims do. Is that good on a Mission compound?"

"Don't interfere with him," I cautioned. "Just join me in praying that God may show him that only Jesus can save him."

This went on for several weeks and then a strange thing happened. At that time we still had three Qua Iboe boys at Adoru and they sometimes conducted prayers. One morning Fettis tried to teach the little group a verse in Igala. It was Romans 6:23 and as he repeated it he mispronounced the word for death. All the Igalas burst out laughing, but Amodu did not join them. He sat transfixed. In his own Igbirra language that mispronounced word had a different meaning, so the verse sounded to him – "The wages of sin is the dreaded sickness."

Now why should this worry him so much? The reason was that, instead of using the money given him for the canoe journey, he had walked the whole way and saved the fare. He was afraid that, if I found out, he would be in trouble for not returning the money, and that "dreaded disease" was something he feared above all things. In his own wonderful way, the Holy Spirit used a mispronounced word and a troubled conscience to convict him of his need of forgiveness.

"What do you Christians do about sin?" he asked Fettis.

The Qua Iboe boy knew how to help him and that day Amodu put his trust in the Saviour. Just to be sure, he later came to me with the same question and I too explained that, although the wages of sin was death, the free gift of God was eternal life through Jesus Christ our Lord.

Amodu soon got a firm grasp of the Gospel message. He quickly learned English and was ready to interpret for me on my next visit to Bassa. On the first night a great company gathered to hear the word of God through the lips of one of their own sons. We had not gone very far before being interrupted. When I asked what the murmuring was about he replied,

"Because my father was an Igbirra, all the Igbirras here are saying to me, 'You are telling the Bassa people what the white man is saying, but what about us? We don't understand their language'."

"Amodu," I said, "if I give you time could you interpret into Igbirra too?"

"I'll be very happy to do so," he replied cheerfully.

On we went with double interpretation but were soon stopped again. Amodu explained,

"There are many Muslims here who only understand Hausa and they are saying, 'What about us?' "

"Well, what can we do about that?" I asked, "Do you know Hausa?"

To my utter amazement the boy responded,

"Very well, sir."

"If I give you plenty of time, will you pass on the

message to all three groups?"

Obviously enjoying the situation, he said with a laugh,

"I will try, sir."

So that night, as on the day of Pentecost, everyone heard the good news in his mother tongue. How wonderfully God had gifted this boy, and brought us together to fulfil his purposes! From that time on I tried to cross the Benue at three-monthly intervals to bring medical help and the word of God, and always Amodu was by my side to act as "go-between".

It was a great day in 1936 when we were able to introduce the first resident missionary to the Bassas. The local chief had been notified of our coming and was at the beach with his people to greet us as we arrived in a canoe, packed full of loads and helpers. Another twelve miles of rough travelling lay ahead when cycles had to be carried rather than ridden, and it was a weary party that reached our destination as darkness fell. With us was a Qua Iboe teacher and his wife and child – a gallant little family, facing a fearsome venture to bring the Gospel to these unknown people. The following days were spent in a fruitless search for safe drinking water, a problem which later made it necessary to change the location of our Mission centre. I returned to Adoru, the Qua Iboe family was settled nearby, and missionary George Curry was left to begin his devoted service, with Amodu as his interpreter and right-hand man.

Amodu left Bassa to continue his education but eventually returned to become headmaster of the first government school. He was later ordained an elder in Ankpa church and appointed head of The Boys' Brigade in the Northern Provinces. In 1967 he had a year's training at Cliff College in England and went to work with the Sudan Interior Mission in northern

Nigeria. It was one of my regrets that we were unable to meet during my last visit to that land.

In spite of this promising start and the sacrifices of dedicated workers, the story of Bassa has been a discouraging one. Like our car in the sand, each effort to progress has been followed by a reverse, with little to show for much expenditure of energy! George Curry and others after him were forced to retire because of ill-health. Some, designated to the task, never even reached the field.

In 1940 a lovely young primary school teacher heard the call of God and was accepted by the Mission Council. As we were due to return to Nigeria, arrangements were made for her to travel with us, and we were joined at Liverpool by another new missionary from Scotland. We had shopping to do before boarding the steamer for West Africa, so agreed a time to meet for lunch. As my wife and I waited to cross the street to the restaurant, we saw our two young people standing at the entrance. They had eyes for no one but each other and we knew that the die was cast – it was clearly love at first sight!

Now we were well aware of the Mission's attitude to such romances, and were supposed to act as chaperones. Aboard ship we tried to avoid leaving them too often alone but, apart from a gentle caution, we could do no more. They seemed destined for each other.

On arrival, our golden-haired teacher was posted to the Girls' Training School in Qua Iboe, while the young man was located four hundred miles north in Bassa. A few months later it became known that they were engaged and planned to be married on their first furlough in two years' time. As their adopted parents, we invited them to spend part of the school vacation with us, and what a happy time that was for us all! We little guessed the sore trial that lay ahead.

In their second year, we got an urgent message that the girl had developed purpura, a serious illness for which there was then no known remedy. She was being nursed in the doctor's house at Etinan and, as her condition worsened, first her fiancé, then my wife and finally I, myself, joined the prayerful, loving group around her. It was a great shock to see that lovely young life, once so brimful of energy, lying there like a fragile flower.

A doctor from another mission had been called for consultation, but could give no hope. The young missionary from Bassa clung to me in an agony, and it fell to Hilda's lot to break the news to the dying girl. We gathered round her bedside and saw her grief-stricken lover take that delicate hand in his. What, oh what, will we see or hear next? Looking up with a divine calm, she said,

"So I'm not going to join you in Bassa after all. I'm going home to be with Jesus. You must not stay up there alone. You must ask God to bring someone else into your life to take my place."

At her request, we read a psalm and sang –

"And above the rest this note shall swell
My Jesus hath done all things well."

I shall never forget the fragrance in the room that day as the dear girl poured out her love as an offering to her Lord. Two days later we laid the empty house in a grave at Afaha Eket, but the bright spirit had already gone into the presence of the one whom she loved above any earthly friend.

We were not surprised that the young man felt he must seek a fresh start in another mission field, where he was later joined by the partner whom God sent to work alongside him in his harvest. But once again Bassa was bereft.

Over the years there have been many occasions when we have questioned, "Is it worth holding on in this hard field? Would it not be wiser to concentrate our resources on more fruitful places as other societies have done?" But each time we have been held on course by the memory of God's leading to the task, and the confidence that he is still able to move there by the power of the Holy Spirit.

Why has the enemy of souls launched his fiercest attacks upon the missionaries and church in this area? In recent years we have been able to understand his strategy more clearly, for Bassa lies very near to the heartland territory which has been chosen for the new Federal capital of Nigeria. Millions of pounds are being spent on communications, and in 1979 I saw work in progress on great new bridges and roads which will radiate through the whole country from this city of the future. What a strategic position we occupy on the very doorstep of this development! And how we need our dear friends to join us in prayer for God's guidance as we seek his plan for coming days!

Although the churches remain weak we have seen what God can do for Bassa men and women who are given over to him. During my early visits, before they had a resident missionary, I began to notice a small boy from a village a few miles away, who always seemed to know when I had arrived. He stayed around, watching my movements with interest, and found out that I had schools under my management in Igala. He did not attempt to talk to me for I was a white man and he only a small boy, but I was to find out later that he was thinking – "That is a friendly man. If I get to him he might help me to go to school."

After I had returned to Idah from one such visit, a

market lorry drove up to the door of our house. A small figure jumped out and sat down on the steps. Coming out to see what the driver was bringing, I said,

"What can I do for you?"

"This small boy met me at Shiria market in Bassa, about eighty miles away," replied the driver. "He said he wanted to get to Idah and that he had no money but he was sure Mr. Dickson would pay me. Knowing you, sir, I brought him, and there he is."

He pointed to the little fellow who was watching eagerly to see my reaction, although he could not understand what was being said. His only garment was a triangular piece of cloth round his waist, and his complete possessions were tied up in another piece, the size of a large handkerchief. His age would have been about eight years. Having paid the driver, I called an interpreter, and got the following answer to my questions –

"My name is Daniel Turkura and I come from Dimbeku, near Kanyehu. I always see you when you visit us. Please, I want to go to school. There is no school in Bassa so I have come to ask you to help me to go to school here."

I looked into the small upturned face and anxious eyes as he waited for my reply. Then, thinking of the Saviour who loves such little ones, I assured him right away that I would look after him.

During school days Daniel accepted the Lord Jesus as his Saviour and, as the years passed, I heard good reports of him but had little recent contact. In 1979, when staying overnight with missionaries who work independently in another part of Bassa, my host enquired,

"Was it not you who brought up Daniel Turkura?"

"Yes, indeed," I replied, and he went on to tell me

115

about Daniel's academic achievements and the position he now holds as Assistant Registrar at Jos University. I was delighted to hear that he had been helping in many ways with the Bassa language and longed to be able to see him, but had no hope of a meeting as Jos could not be fitted into my itinerary.

The very next day, travelling along that rough road on the way back to Sardauna, a small open lorry suddenly appeared, coming in the opposite direction. The track was so narrow that both vehicles had to slow down and negotiate carefully to pass unscathed. My missionary companion recognised someone in the lorry and began talking to him. Then he spotted another passenger and cried out,

"Daniel Turkura, where have you come from? Do you see who is with me – Mr. Dickson?"

Before I had time to realise what was happening, there was Daniel at my side, ecstatic with delight. I could not describe the joy of that brief meeting. Suddenly Daniel broke away and ran to his transport. In a few seconds he returned and pressed something into my hand, saying,

"Baba, I have no present to give you, but please take this and buy one for yourself."

What a thrilling encounter! Who but the Lord could have timed that meeting in the heart of the Bassa bush to give his children the pleasure of looking into each other's face once more? And cannot that same mighty Lord, who has done so much for Daniel, yet build a strong, pure church to the glory of his name in that needy place?

CHAPTER TEN

Partings

Yes, the old church was still there and looking as lovely as ever among the trees in the spacious compound of Ochadamu Medical Centre. As we walked over for morning service, I admired once again the well-proportioned building, with its white-washed mud walls and high-pitched thatched roof.

Inside, the patients from the Leprosy and General wards and Maternity Unit were assembling to worship the God who had brought this place into being some thirty years ago. Beside me on the platform to help with interpretation, was my old friend, Jacob Achema, recently bereaved of a beloved son but faithfully serving the Lord in the dispensary and as an elder in the church. And there on the wall behind us was the commemorative plâque, bearing a very familiar inscription:

"FROM THE SHORE STREET MISSION,
PORT GLASGOW."

The story of Ochadamu really begins away back in our early days in Igala, when my wife and I first realised the plight of leprosy sufferers for whom no treatment was available. The nearest doctor had reported no leprosy in the area, but we met cases on all our journeys and felt sure that the disease was widespread. Sometimes those afflicted came to our dispensary at Adoru and begged to be allowed to stay on the Mission compound. Permission was given to about eight of them to occupy a few empty houses but, as their number grew and others were afraid to live beside them, we had to ask them to leave. Unable to return home, they built little shacks as near to us as possible and we did what we could to make them comfortable.

One day after we had moved to Idah, Hilda and I were returning home in our little van when we saw a figure lying at the side of the road. Getting out to investigate, we found a man, obviously exhausted and ill. We managed to get him into the van and brought him to our compound, only to discover that he had advanced leprosy. For many days he had been struggling painfully along the road in an effort to reach Idah Government Hospital. When we took him there the African doctor confirmed our diagnosis and notified the authorities.

Word got around that this man was being helped and soon quite a group of similar sufferers were living in shelters near our house. There was not a Christian among them and they were very dejected. We tried to visit them regularly and they brightened considerably, one little girl always running to meet us just because we had given her a brightly-coloured Christmas card. Our hearts went out to these people. Jesus would not have passed them by. But we were stretched to the limit with growing commitments and a shortage of missionaries. All we could do was ask friends to join us in urgent prayer for a doctor and, in the meantime, send twenty patients for treatment to the Church of Scotland settlement at Calabar, over three hundred miles away.

It was 1949 when Dr. Jack Kearney joined us in Igala with his wife and two young sons, one of whom is now himself a Qua Iboe missionary. Immediately we began to lay plans for leprosy clinics and, right from the outset, God's blessing was on the venture.

We noticed that the man in whose house we slept during our preparations was listening very attentively to the gospel message. On a later visit he asked more questions about the way of salvation, and Dr. Kearney and his helper had the joy of introducing him to the Saviour.

The opening of the first clinic created a great sensation. After a feast of yam, fish and garri provided by local church people, I told the expectant crowd, "It is God who has put it into the hearts of his children to help you. He is able not only to heal your sickness but give you new life through Jesus Christ."

Among the doctor's four helpers was an Igala boy whom we had sent three years previously to the leprosy settlement which our own mission had opened in Qua Iboe. Now, restored in health, committed to Christ, and able to read his Igala New Testament, he had returned to help his own people. With him came a gift of £4 from leprosy patients at Ekpene Obom as a token of love for their fellow sufferers in the north. A new day of hope was dawning for them and I can still recall the gratitude and amazement on their faces as they heard of this gift.

The leprosy clinic which opened with forty-two patients, increased within a week to sixty-three. From all over the country they came, and we began to realise the influence these people could have if they eventually returned to their homes, healed and transformed by the power of God.

Three years later, Hilda and I took part in a most thrilling service, arranged to mark the discharge of seven symptom-free patients from the leprosy centre at Ochadamu. By that time, Dr. Bill Holley had taken over from Dr. Kearney; a fine site had been secured for a permanent settlement, and over three hundred leprosy patients were being cared for in simple but adequate buildings.

So many non-leprous patients had come for treatment that it was essential to erect a separate dispensary for them, and a church was also needed to accommodate the growing congregation of worshippers. The estimated cost of both amounted to £600. Earnest prayer was made for this money and the first part of the answer came in an anonymous gift of £500. We were in Scotland just then and one evening, when visiting, I was handed an envelope containing a cheque. It was from the trustees of the Shore Street Mission, founded by my father so many years before. This work had now closed down and, after settling all the debts, it had been decided that the residue should be given to some special project with which I was associated in Nigeria. It amounted to exactly £100.

When the church was completed a simple plâque was placed on its wall to commemorate the good folk of Port Glasgow who, over the years, had prayed so faithfully and given so generously for the work of God in Nigeria. Here it was now looking down upon us at that first discharge day service.

Everyone had worked hard to prepare for the great day, cutting grass, re-plastering the mud houses and putting the finishing touches to the church. The fifteen school children were arrayed in new clothes and all the older patients had washed and mended their best garments for the occasion. With other missionaries we had arrived early and were there to welcome the Attah 'Gala and nine councillors in their turban head-dresses and flowing robes. After inspecting the patients' quarters they returned to meet the District Officer, other government officials, and traders from Idah.

The church was already filled to capacity, with many folk outside, when we took our seats on the big semi-circular platform which had been beautifully decorated with flowers. During the service which followed, the D.O. spoke appreciatively of our Mission's work and the Attah 'Gala presented Discharge Cards to five men and two women. All eyes were fixed on him as this was the first time he had looked on a leprosy sufferer – a sight strictly forbidden to his predecessors. It was then my great privilege to pass on a brief message, explaining how those returning home could best show their thankfulness to God by trusting his Son and showing love to their fellows.

Next day was Sunday, with further services of thanksgiving, and it seemed as if the people could not do enough to show their gratitude. One of the discharged women distributed gifts of food among the friends whom she would soon be leaving. In return they gathered their pennies and halfpennies and gave her a total of seven shillings and ninepence. But at the afternoon service she brought it to Dr. Holley, saying,

"I cannot take this money. God has been so good to me, I now give it back to him."

Before leaving, this woman came up with others to the doctor's house for a final greeting. The doctor's wife was there with her baby in her arms and the woman reached out to take the child. Just for a moment the mother hesitated. Then with a smile she gave her precious infant into the hands that still bore the scars of leprosy. It could not have been an easy thing to do, but the look on the faces of those people made it worthwhile.

"Now we know we are really clean," it seemed to say. "If Doctor's wife had thought there was any risk she would not have given her the child."

It was now thirty years since I had arrived in Nigeria. Hilda had preceded me and had been giving of herself without limit. It was clear that her strength was almost exhausted, so, with great reluctance, we decided to retire from the field. Only a deep consciousness of being in the will of God, and the comfort of leaving our work in the capable hands of John and Janet Neal, carried us through the painful partings of October 1953. As we left Idah, a poor woman thrust nine pennies into my wife's hand to buy oranges for refreshment on the journey, while the Christian women did their best to console the sobbing children to whom we had been parents. Never would we forget the generosity and love of our African friends.

On our way to the coast we spent a few days at Ikot Edong where crowds of people came to greet us, including our Adiaha, carried with her three children on the back of her husband's bicycle! During our short time there, two elders who had not spoken for years were reconciled and on the following Sunday each publicly acknowledged his fault and change of heart.

Retirement for us did not mean inactivity. Indeed we liked to think of it as re-tyre-ment, for we were to serve in a new capacity as the Qua Iboe Mission's representatives in Scotland. God wonderfully provided a little flat for us in Glasgow, where we were able to entertain many visitors, both black and white.

Two weeks after moving in we had the thrill of welcoming one of our Igala "sons," then on vacation from London University. Some twenty years previously, a little scrap of humanity whose life was in danger had been brought to the Mission compound, where he was fed, clothed and mothered. In return he helped with the chores and was always at hand to interpret for "Iye," until she became fluent in Igala and needed assistance only for public speaking.

He was an intelligent boy and quickly absorbed all the education then available in Idah. We could see his ability and decided to send him south to our Boys' Institute at Etinan. From there he went on to a government teacher training centre, and later returned to Idah school as assistant headmaster. He had a good influence upon the young people and under his leadership the boys' section of the Sunday School made remarkable progress.

What joy, then, to welcome Daniel Enefola on his arrival in Glasgow aboard the 'Royal Scot'! That evening he carefully observed all that was done about the kitchen and next morning we emerged from our bedroom to find the fire kindled and breakfast already prepared. He thought of many ways to show his loving regard, and it warmed our hearts to have him with us once again.

Daniel's second visit coincided with the Kelvin Hall Crusade and, night after night, he joined us to hear Dr. Billy Graham proclaim the Saviour whom he had trusted as a schoolboy in Idah. Before leaving London to supervise Q.I.M. schools in Igala, he 'phoned to say good-bye. At the end of the call he added modestly,

"Baba, you will be pleased to know that in our final examination here I tied for first place with another student."

Mr. Enefola later graduated in the U.S.A. and returned to become the first African principal of our secondary school at Ochaja. During my recent tour I visited him in another mixed secondary school to which he had been transferred, and since then he has been promoted to the Education Headquarters for

Benue State at Makurdi. What possibilities lay hidden in that little life which God entrusted to our protection all those years ago!

Well, we settled down happily to life in Scotland, addressing many meetings, encouraging prayer and keeping in touch with many friends of the Mission. One of the lovely things about being a missionary is the family spirit that unites you with fellow-workers and home supporters. All over Britain I still have former colleagues who are like brothers and sisters – and what reminiscences when we meet!

But this oneness is not limited to old friends. The Lord of the harvest is still sending forth more labourers and sometimes he allows us to share in the process. Two young nurses sat one evening in their Bible Training College, facing the challenge of Igala's need. One recognised the call of God and responded without hesitation. The other was uncertain and afraid of being influenced. Some time later, at the close of a meeting, she noticed my wife and me leaving the hall and thought, with relief,

"I'm near the end of the queue. They will be out before I reach the door."

She got there, however, only to find us standing alone as the crowd passed by. Suddenly she felt she must speak to us and came forward to introduce herself. From that day on she had our constant prayers and the assurance that, as Hilda said,

"If you come to tell us that God is calling you to South America we'll be just as glad as if it were Qua Iboe! Our joy and yours is to be in his will."

Both those girls eventually went to nurse at Ochadamu, strong in the knowledge that God alone had chosen them and would equip them for the task.

August 1956 found us on holiday in Warrenpoint, a quiet seaside town in the Mourne area of Co. Down, with my wife's two sisters, brother-in-law, and another life-long friend. Hilda was in great form. Always a good walker, she roamed around like a young person, enjoying everything, and often exclaiming,

"Isn't it lovely to have this holiday all together?"

On the morning of Wednesday 8th we went a little way into the country by car and then got out to walk. It was a beautiful day. As we strolled along the unspoiled lanes, Hilda would sometimes get into conversation with a friendly passer-by and, in her natural way, offered one of the little booklets she always carried in her handbag.

At lunch we decided that this would be a good afternoon to spend on Fiddlers' Green, a little elevated plot of grass among the trees overlooking Carlingford Lough. Carrying books and rugs, we set out up the winding path. Three of the party went on ahead while we followed more slowly, pausing several times to rest and admire the widening view of sea and mountain scenery. Hilda and I were the last to arrive and as we walked toward the others she called out,

"Is this the place?"

"Yes," came the reply, "this is it."

We sat down beside our friends, at the end of the row nearest the lough, and Hilda lay back to relax before opening her book. We heard a little choking sound and turned round quickly to see what was wrong.

How can I describe that awful moment? Artificial respiration was applied until a doctor arrived, but I knew, and felt the others did too, that my beloved had been called from the joy of being with her loved ones, to the eternal bliss of the Saviour's presence.

What a wonderful homegoing for one whose only thought was to please him! I, who for all those years had walked beside her through forest, bush and swamp, knew how closely she walked with God. Now, like Enoch, she was not, for God had taken her home. I could only thank him for his great gift to me, and leave the future in his hands.

In spite of the awful shock and loss, life had to go on, and I was very conscious of divine help as I readjusted to life on my own. Letters began coming from Nigeria, telling of the grief and tears with which the unexpected news had been received. Nine years previously, we had had the joy of welcoming into the ranks of the Mission my wife's niece, Dr. Esther Davis. Word of her aunt's death reached her on temporary duty at Ochadamu, while she was actually holding a clinic at Idah where Hilda helped so many sick folk. With her, in the providence of God, was Norah Curran, one of the young nurses who had just arrived from Glasgow, and Pastor Joseph Okpanachi.

Among the many Nigerians who felt a keen sense of personal loss was an elder of Idah church, Hon. Peter Achimugu, who wrote at the end of a wonderful tribute:

"The name of Iye Dickson, so calm, gentle and gracious, will ring for generations in the hearts and memories of many men and women who loved her and are longing to meet her at the Saviour's feet."

Interest in the Mission was growing in Scotland and there was plenty to keep me busy, but Nigeria was never far from my thoughts and it was like a tonic, in 1959, to hear that I was to have a visit from Peter Achimugu. My first contact with Peter had taken place soon after our arrival in Igala, when we were travelling around in our little Austin seven. The roads were only in the making and on the job was a small steam roller, fired with wood which was cut from the surrounding bush and left in bundles along the verges. I used to stop and chat to the man in charge and found him very friendly. He told me that in his younger days he was taken down to Ibo country as a house servant. While there he attended a Bible class conducted by Archdeacon Wilcox of the Church Missionary Society, but he seemed to remember little of what had been taught.

Peter was a good listener and, as we talked from time to time, the Holy Spirit was revealing to him the truth about God's love and salvation. One day he appeared at Idah Mission house, all aglow and excited, to tell me,

"I now understand clearly that when Jesus died on the cross he died for me and I want to accept him as my Saviour."

I took him into the bedroom and, as we knelt there, the great transaction took place. What a momentous event that proved to be for Peter and for his people! In 1944 I wrote about him:

"Our stalwart in the church in Idah is Peter Achimugu. He is of middle age, an earnest Christian and greatly trusted by his employers. This week has seen some changes in tribal affairs. Three councillors have been deposed and Peter now occupies a leading position under the Attah, having accepted the office on condition that he would not be asked to take part in heathen customs and ceremonies. He is superintendent of the Sunday School and we hope he will become one of the first elders to be ordained in the Igala church."

When Nigeria was granted a measure of self-government, Peter was a member of the Northern House of Assembly. He was then appointed to the first Cabinet in Northern Nigeria, and chosen to represent his country at the coronation of Queen Elizabeth. From London he wrote to the Mission headquarters in Belfast:

"I was in Westminster Abbey when her Majesty kissed the Bible and promised to rule her people in justice before God. I believe she will be a great Queen, God helping her . . . With regard to myself in the Cabinet, I trust God for his guidance, wisdom and knowledge, for I have no book knowledge and no experience in statesmanship. I know my Lord is with me and many friends are praying."

By the time Hon. Peter Achimugu came to stay with me in 1959, he was further honoured by being made a member of the Nigerian Privy Council and invested with the Order of the British Empire. He had been working extremely hard and was sent to Britain to get a complete rest, away from the constant demands made upon him in Nigeria. As I awaited his arrival I wondered – "Will he be changed? Will all this prominence have made him proud?" But my friend was just the same humble, warm-hearted Peter who had knelt beside me in Idah Mission House – a truly great and good man.

It was Peter Achimugu who had helped us to acquire an ideal site for our leprosy settlement and, down through the years, he took a deep interest in its development. Soon after visiting me in Glasgow, he presided over a big crowd of Africans and Europeans, gathered at Ochadamu for the opening of a modern maternity unit, by another of my wife's beloved nieces, who was then on short-term service with the Mission. A simple plâque beside the entrance links it with the one who, day and night for many years, was on call to help the mothers and babies of Igala.

THE HILDA DICKSON MATERNITY UNIT
OPENED 5th DECEMBER 1959
BY DR. ALICE DAVIS
"LOVE NEVER FAILETH"

CHAPTER ELEVEN

Back To The Front!

The last day of an old year is always a time for looking back and Sunday 31st December, 1978 was no exception. Arriving by car at Ankpa for the morning service, I recalled my first cross-country trek from Adoru to this important place, with its big market and strong Muslim community. After several visits in the early 1930's we were able to locate a Qua Iboe teacher there and he was followed in later years by several missionaries. My most vivid memories, however, date from the 1960's.

I often warn new missionaries, "Be careful; before you know it, Africa will have stolen your heart," for this has been my own experience. After my wife's death I longed more than ever to return to Nigeria for another term of service, but no one could be found to take my place in Scotland, so I had to be content with a couple of prolonged visits to the land of my adoption, which will be mentioned in our next chapter.

It was in 1964 that the invitation came to relieve Mervyn Crooks as principal of the recently-established Church Training Centre at Ankpa. With great joy I set off once more, little dreaming how literally "front-line" my new assignment would prove to be.

The twenty students were a happy, hard-working bunch of men, all of whom had already served as preachers in Igala churches. I can picture them bent over their books, enjoying a lively game of football or singing heartily under a moonlit sky to the accompaniment of my accordion. They were divided into English and Igala-speaking classes and I had the help of an African tutor and, later, a new missionary couple, who for a time had shared my flat in Glasgow. After their one-year course some students went on to our Bible College in the south, and in 1978 I was glad to renew fellowship with many of these in the city churches and pioneer situations where they are now serving the Lord. It was also very satisfying to see the preparations being made at Ankpa for the re-opening of a new, up-graded college where future Igala preachers can be given a more adequate Bible training to meet the demands of the 1980's.

It was in 1966 that we began to realise that serious trouble was brewing in Nigeria. Reports of police action in Ibo territory were followed by a declaration of independence for the Eastern Region, under the name of "Biafra". As well as the strong Ibo tribe, this region included some smaller groups who were opposed to secession and we were concerned for their welfare and that of our missionaries working among them in the old Qua Iboe field. I went on furlough that year and arrived back just after the flight of the Easterners who escaped death in the Northern massacre. The war was now on.

On the fifth of June 1967, my little radio brought news of the evacuation of eight hundred Americans, seventy French citizens and a number of Britishers, but there was no word of our friends in the south. We were in Federal territory and the border was only twenty-five miles from Ankpa, so Igala division was declared a danger area and the British High Commissioner advised all missionaries to clear out, as he would not be responsible for their safety. Next day our missionaries left for Jos, having handed over their duties, as far as possible, to African helpers.

The students at the Church Training Centre had asked permission to return to their homes, leaving me free to make my own decision, and as I was seeking God's guidance who should arrive but the local government officer. He was friendly and symphetic.

"If I close my dispensary what provision will there be for the people?" I enquired.

"All government supplies are going to the forces," he replied. "If you go, there will be no medical help throughout the whole area."

"In spite of the High Commissioner's advice I feel I should stay. I'm the senior member of our Mission here and I've no family responsibilities, but I would like your opinion."

"The people are already excited," confessed the officer. "They know you, and as long as you stay there will be some measure of calm. If you go it will be much harder to avoid panic."

So, with an assurance of help in any emergency, he left me confirmed in my decision to remain in Ankpa and give what assistance I could in this hour of need. Friends at home were concerned about my safety, so I wrote to the Mission's Honorary Secretary,

"I am not a hero and have no desire to be a voluntary martyr, so do not be over-anxious about me. I'm as happy as anyone could be and never have a dull moment."

That was literally true!

Petrol was scarce but I tried to pay a weekly visit to the various centres now without missionary help. My arrival at Ochadamu was greeted with great delight as it was thought I had gone north with the others. As I passed down the wards, the patients clapped their hands with gladness, and my presence gave the nurses authority to resume some treatments that had been stopped. After doing a ward round one day, John Atabo, who was in charge, remarked quietly,

"There is a patient waiting for you in the theatre."

Not wanting to lose the confidence of my helpers, I hid my fears and followed him praying inwardly that the case might be within my limited scope. The patient was already on the operating table and two nurses stood beside him, already gowned and waiting for the "surgeon". With my heart in my mouth, I went to see what the job might entail and was relieved to find an abcess from a diseased gland in the neck. So I "scrubbed up" and, while John gave the anaesthetic, I chose a scalpel, cleaned out the cavity and gave directions about the dressing. Imagine my feelings as I left the theatre, when John looked at me and said,

"Baba, I thought it was only your wife who had done medical work!"

During the six weeks' absence of my fellow-missionaries, my most anxious time was when I developed malaria. The attack was more severe than usual, probably because my resistance had been lowered by a certain amount of strain, but after perspiring freely all night I felt much better, though it was some days before my legs regained their steadiness. Needless to say it was a great comfort to welcome back the evacuees early in August.

Fighting had moved farther from us, but Ankpa was on the main road to the "Biafran" capital and big convoys of Federal soldiers stayed overnight before leaving on the last lap of their journey. This provided a fine opportunity to distribute literature, and the Scripture Gift Mission were generous in supplying booklets in Hausa, Arabic, English and Igala. Soldiers would crowd around me with outstretched hands, and my heart went out in prayer that God would bless his word to these young men, many of whom would never return to their homes again.

On Christmas Day 1967 all available accommodation at Ochadamu was commandeered by the troops and here too I found an eagerness for the Scriptures in various languages. There were many Christians in this contingent and up to fifty soldiers attended prayer meetings during their brief stay. How surprised I would have been in that army tent in France, if I could have looked forward over fifty years and seen myself helping to bring comfort to soldiers in Nigeria!

These were busy months. Our dispensary at Ankpa was going strong six days a week. Bible training had resumed and the students were trying to make up for lost time. Every Sunday they went out to churches that had no preachers and their efforts met with an encouraging response. At Inye a number of prayer groups were formed and within three months over eighty new people began to attend the services. This growth continued under the ministry of a former student and tutor, Nathaniel Egwu, who was still serving faithfully when I addressed a thousand worshippers in that church on the last day of 1978.

Travel was not easy during the emergency. Some congregations met very near the border and to visit these danger zones a permit had to be obtained from the government officer. On one occasion a bridge had been mined and the military removed their explosives so that I might pass over safely to conduct a communion service. Road blocks also created considerable problems. Returning one day from Ochadamu I found the barrier already down at Anyigba. As Idah closed at 7 p.m. and it was now a few minutes past six, I decided this must be down for the checking of lorries. My car could pass under the bar so I went on, saying to the boy beside me,

"If we hurry we can reach the Ankpa barrier before it goes down at seven."

Three minutes before the hour we arrived to find it closed.

"Look here," I tackled the guard, "why is your barrier down before time?"

He looked at his watch and replied,

"It is three minutes to seven. This barrier goes down at 6 p.m."

"Well," I reasoned, "how am I to know that, when Idah closes at seven?"

He laughed good-humouredly.

"Don't worry, Baba," he said, lifting the bar to let me through, satisfied that our toubles were over.

At the turning of the road to my house we encountered another barrier and a stranger on guard with his rifle at the ready. He glowered at me and asked many questions, checking every statement with my boy. At last he allowed us through, and glad we were to be safely home again. However, I was unhappy about having broken the law by passing under the barrier at Anyigba, so I typed a letter of apology and sent it to the Police Office there. Next time when passing that way I dropped in to see the sergeant. He called another officer and as they joked together, he explained,

"When we got your letter we just said, 'What other white man would have written to us like this.' There is no trouble, Baba, for we know you would not want to break the law."

I have found that when I treat my African brothers with respect and courtesy, they usually respond in the same manner, and in this way I was able to keep on good terms with those in authority during difficult days.

This was also a time for proving the over-ruling

power of God in unexpected situations. My residence permit was due for renewal and I had been commissioned to get one for a missionary nurse who was urgently needed in Bassa. These permits could only be issued in Lagos so I took the first available opportunity of transport to the Federal capital to visit the immigration authorities. When I asked for the nurse's permit the official looked up the dossier and said,

"This lady has been working in Biafra."

"Yes," I agreed, "but she went home to Ireland and now we want her to relieve another nurse in Bassa Komo."

"No one who has been in that area will be allowed into the North," he said firmly, and no amount of persuasion could make him change his mind.

What was I to do? Knowing that many people in Britain and Nigeria were praying about this permit I directed an urgent "telegram" to the heavenly Father, in whose business I was engaged. At the same time I handed my passport to the official, saying,

"Here is my own for renewal, please."

He passed it over to two juniors who examined it, made some comment to each other, and then laid it on the desk before their senior officer.

"There's something wrong with this man's passport," they said, pointing to the year of my birth.

Looking over the counter, I enquired what was amiss.

"Your date of birth is down here as 1894", they replied.

"Well, what's wrong with that?" I asked, rather enjoying the situation.

"Is that really the year you were born?"

"Yes, and I came to Nigeria in 1922."

That broke the ice! They burst out laughing and I

knew my prayer was answered. Everything else was forgotten as they asked about their country in those early days, exclaiming in astonishment,

"We were not even born then!"

The atmosphere had changed now and when the juniors finally left I felt able to re-open the matter of the nurse's permit. This time the official kindly told me how to go about getting it, and before long that missionary was back again in Nigeria. Thank God for a "hot-line" to heaven in time of need!

News had been reaching us about the sufferings of the Ibaji people at the hands of marauding troops, and I determined to pay them a visit at the earliest possible opportunity. Twelve border villages had been looted and burned. Some of their inhabitants had escaped to safer places where they were given land to farm, but they were going to be very short of food until harvest time and many of them were undernourished and sick. The need was made known and, with a grant from Home Council and gifts from personal friends, a relief fund was quickly set up.

Permission had to be sought from three different sources, including the military, and this was granted early in December. So, when the Bible school closed for the Christmas vacation, I moved to Idah to plan the operation.

With the help of Ibaji church elders, the people were gathered into three centres and I spent about six days in each, working from dawn till dark to give free treatment to the sick. In spite of the fact that many more were still hiding in the forest, my helpers and I treated no less than eleven hundred adults and six hundred and thirty-five children. After paying for the medicines, there was enough money left to give £60 to each of the stricken villages. It was not a large sum, but the people were encouraged and comforted by the knowledge that Christians overseas were thinking of them in their distress.

Picture the scene as one village shared out its gift. The people gathered round, their bodies thin under ragged clothing but their faces shining with anticipation, while the headmen spread little sticks on the ground, one to represent each family, with smaller sticks to represent the children. A small amount was allocated to each stick, and in this way the money was divided to the satisfaction of all. The touching gratitude of chiefs and people provided a wonderful opportunity to commend God's great gift in Jesus Christ our Lord.

As so often happens, there was a sudden descent from the sublime to the ridiculous for I arrived back at Idah beach to face arrest! A very officious N.C.O. refused to recognise my permits and accused me of selling medicines to the "Biafrans". With his gun in my side and smelling strongly of alcohol, he poured out all sorts of accusations and would not allow me to speak.

"Get all your loads into this lorry," he commanded. "I'm taking you to my captain."

Now the beach was a mile away from Idah mission house and I had been wondering how I could get there with so much luggage. Was this going to be another of God's surprises?

When at last I managed to get a word in edgeways, I warned him,

"You are only putting yourself into trouble. Your captain already knows all about my movements."

"Yes," chimed in another soldier, "I accompanied this man to see the captain."

The N.C.O. was obviously taken aback and handed me my permits, saying with an uneasy laugh,

"You take your loads out of the lorry and go."

137

"Oh no," the canny Scot replied, "you told me to put them there to go to the captain and I'm not taking them out again."

For a moment he was speechless. Then he called a driver and ordered,

"Take this man to his house."

"To the captain first," I added firmly, and to the captain we went.

He was furious and imprisoned the N.C.O. for the night as a last warning before being reduced to the ranks. I had no wish to get the man into trouble but felt it was right that the relief operation should be vindicated in the eyes of the many spectators. So it was, that missionary, boys and baggage eventually reached home in safety and style, under military protection!

By May 1969 I was very ready for furlough and so great was the demand for a first-hand account of events in Nigeria that I did not get back again for a full year. By then the fighting was over, but strict regulations were still in force and as our steamer docked at Lagos the loudspeaker blared out,

"The military are in charge of everything and all orders will be from them."

I had a lot of boxes to clear with the customs, as many friends had sent gifts of clothing for relief purposes. Some of these got through without trouble, but others had been on a different steamer and were still missing. While awaiting their arrival I decided to look up the Military Commandant, who had often been in our house when he was a boy at school in Idah. It was hard to get anyone to show me his office for he was greatly feared by his staff. However, after explaining to the military police, I was allowed to enter and found him busy at his desk.

"Good afternoon, Colonel," I said.

The imposing khaki-clad figure looked up, then rising to his feet he said in amazement,

"Mr. Dickson, this is wonderful. Where have you come from?"

He was like a schoolboy again with delight, and introduced me to some shipping officials. I could see that he was busy and said I only called to give him greetings, but he enquired my business in Lagos and, before I knew what was happening, he had called the shipping agent, and ordered him to get my loads through at once and transport me to wherever I was staying. All bills of expense were to be sent to him.

Well, Lagos docks and Customs sheds were never so quickly cleared as when this poor man took over the job! Running hither and thither, he kept repeating with agitation –

"It is the Commandant's order! It is the Commandant's order!"

As no other vehicle was available I ended up being driven through the crowded Lagos streets in the Commandant's own minibus, its siren bleeping to clear a route all the way to S.I.M. Guest House, where my arrival caused quite a commotion!

The aftermath of civil war is never easy and we were very concerned about the coming together again of the Qua Iboe Church. Twenty per cent of its six hundred and fifty congregations were in the Ibo country and completely cut off by the secession. How were they faring? Would the different tribes ever again be able to work and worship harmoniously in one fellowship?

The first approach was made when the Igala Church sent a delegation with £200 worth of foodstuffs for their Ibo brothers. What a reception was given to the drivers of these vehicles, piled high with yams, beans and garri! It was a good beginning.

Soon after arriving back from furlough, I set out with our missionary, Robert Thompson, to bring further help to what were then the South-Eastern and East Central States. One of our doctors and a missionary nurse had been seconded to work with a Red Cross relief team and we stayed overnight with them before going on to Aba. What a sight met our eyes there! The church had a large shell hole in the pulpit, many of the stained-glass windows were broken, all the lights were ripped out and most of the pews gone. The Mission house was destroyed. The secondary school had no desks, forms, paper or pencils. Yet the headmaster was bravely preparing to enroll pupils the following day.

Like all their people, our pastors and church leaders were practically destitute, and pathetically grateful for gifts of clothing and money. We had brought lovely new Bibles for the pastors and Mr. Irondi, our former headmaster at Idah who, prior to the war, had been Secretary of the Qua Iboe Church Conference. The sufferings of the past years had left their mark on these good men. They had seen members of their families and flocks mown down in the fighting or succumbing to disease or starvation, yet their faith burned brightly and, with limited strength, they were attempting to gather their scattered congregations. We had been given money to purchase bicycles for them, but where to get these was the problem. The Ibos were still afraid to venture outside their own area so we offered to see what we could do in the S.E. State.

We reached Etinan hospital on the Tuesday night and were warmly welcomed by our missionaries who, after trying experiences, were back on duty once more. Further gifts of money and clothing were distributed. One tea-chest went to the Leprosy

Hospital where Bassey Ette had nobly carried on the work while separated from his wife and family, one of whom never returned from the conflict. Rations had been extremely scarce and nothing but his faith in God had enabled this dear man to stay at his post and care for his patients. Another tea-chest was destined for the orphanage, which women of the church had set up to cater for over fifty children who had been left without close relatives. It was moving to see how efficiently and lovingly these little ones were being "mothered" by some whom we ourselves had cared for in days gone by.

But where were we going to get those promised bicycles? We were told they were impossible to obtain. When eventually some were discovered in Port Harcourt the agent stipulated,

"We can only sell one at a time. They are so scarce that people have been buying to sell again in the market at big prices."

I had visions of returning to Ibo country with one bicycle and trying to decide which of those needy pastors would get it. I thought too of the people whose generous gifts had made the purchase possible. Surely this was a time for using that heavenly "hot-line", so, with hearts lifted to God, we tried to explain the situation and plead for a special concession.

"Very well," the agent said at last, "if you can guarantee that you will personally deliver these cycles to the rightful owners I will let you have all I've got at a reduced rate."

At a reduced rate! My, this was "exceeding abundant"! So off we went with seventeen brand-new bicycles, which were soon carrying their grateful riders far and wide on missions of mercy. Before leaving Aba we had a meeting at which I spoke of the opportunities of the hour, and writing home later I expressed the conviction that the Ibo church would accept this challenge.

Such faith was amply justified. When I paid a brief return visit at the end of 1978 to attend the Qua Iboe Church Conference at Aba, delegates from every tribe met together for worship and business in that once devastated church, restored to its former beauty, and now the centre of a thrilling evangelistic ministry. From it, eager young Christians are going out into the streets at 5 a.m. to witness to crowds of people who, even at that early hour, throng the streets of this busy township. In the church vestry, the pastor prays for them and waits to counsel the many inquirers who are directed to him for help. Without any resident missionaries, and cast upon God alone, the Christians in Ibo land have triumphed over their sufferings.

CHAPTER TWELVE

In The Swamps

"Such a thrill after a good night to wake up and know I'm in Ibaji!" This was the entry in my diary for 5th January 1979. The previous day we had been driven in the Ochadamu land-rover over the new road along the eastern bank of the Niger. It was a hot, bumpy and dusty journey, with four of us crammed into the front seat, but aching bones were soon forgotten in the warmth of our welcome at Unale.

My fellow-passengers were Dr. Derek Belgrave and his bride, whom he was bringing for the first time to Ibaji. After many greetings and the presentation of a large duck they left us to continue their journey to Enweli, where I was to join them in a few days' time. Meanwhile I was the guest of my former house-boy and friend, James Odekwe. It was good to see "Big James" again, standing six feet tall in flowing Igala robe and hat, his face beaming with delight at our reunion.

We had a lot to talk about for, after working with the first Qua Iboe teacher to be stationed in Ibaji, James had come to live with us in Idah. He brought his prospective bride to be trained by my wife and later helped me in his own home district. James is respected in the community, and played a big part in persuading the government to provide Ibaji's first road, along which we had just travelled.

My first visit to this isolated, swampy area, southwest of Adoru, had been made with Hilda in February 1933, in a barge lent to us by the District

Officer. Eight men, perched in the fore part, poled us through shallow water as it was dry season and the river was low. After five hours we stepped ashore into an experience that we were never to forget.

News of our coming had already reached the Onu, who was waiting with his headmen to greet us. Taking off his sandals he prostrated himself in the usual salutation. I explained our desire to help their sick folk and tell them about the living God.

"It is good," he responded courteously and led the way to the nearby government rest house, to the accompaniment of drums and a flute-like instrument that reminded us of the bag-pipes tuning up! That night the people of Onyedega listened attentively to the Gospel message. Next day we held a clinic, a women's meeting and an evening lantern service, before trekking a further six miles to the larger town of Unale.

We were well used to the signs of spirit worship but never before had we seen so many as here. Every tree and dwelling had some kind of ju-ju. Many of the idols were in little houses, protected by a fence and only brought out for special occasions, when singers and dancers performed in their honour before crowds of spectators. At first only the headmen ventured near us as no white person had been seen there before, except the government officer who came about once a year accompanied by armed policemen. Fear gradually melted as we moved from place to place and sat among them on low stools, taking an interest in their families and telling Good News.

On the Saturday night we reached another village and encountered a procession, singing wildly and carrying a huge ju-ju and many laden baskets, on the way to a big sacrifice. We managed to find the headman who showed us an empty house where we could stay till Monday, but, although we were very tired, there was little sleep that night for a heathen play was in progress and all the men were drunk with corn wine. In the oppressive darkness, heat and din we lay praying that God would sober them enough to listen to his word the next day. Sure enough, that service turned out to be one of the best of our entire sixteen days' trek.

Everywhere we were welcomed for our medical work, but were often made to understand that the word of God and schools were not required. They had their own gods, and anyone who forsook the village customs would be cut off from his people or suffer persecution. The enemy of souls had his defences in good repair to withstand the coming of the Gospel.

Over the years, as other duties permitted, we visited Ibaji with our medicines and our message, gladly accepting the dust and dirt, the difficulties of travel and the lack of privacy, for the privilege of showing God's love to these needy people, but we were painfully aware that all we could do was a mere drop in the bucket. Even after we retired the situation continued to haunt us. It was not until four years after my wife's death that the opportunity arose to fulfil my great desire to actully live amongst the Ibajis.

I was paying a return visit to Igala in 1960 when I learned that the new Mission house at Enweli was likely to be left unoccupied when Alec and Hilda Gillies and their little daughter returned home to Scotland. It had been a big achievement to get this little house built on one of the few sites that lay above flood level, all the materials being carried down by canoe and head loads from Idah. For the first time, the people had had their own missionaries. Now that costly house was to be left empty. Could I persuade

Home Council to let me take over for a while?

After prayerful consultation the Field executive sent home an urgent cable – "IMPERATIVE DICKSON OCCUPY IBAJI". I waited eagerly for a reply and, oh, what joy when the answer arrived – "PERMISSION GRANTED"! It would take a whole book to describe my experiences in Ibaji, so I can only pick out some of the most vivid memories of our early contacts, of that relief period in 1960–61, and of the later years when I was located in Enweli between 1970 and 1973.

Life in Ibaji was unlike any of our previous locations. For about two months of every year most of the land lay under flood water from the river Niger. The people prepared for the floods by erecting platforms in their houses, on which they could live and sleep, and canoes, moored to the doorposts, were used for moving around. Most of these leaked a little and every dip or lurch shipped a small sea, but only strangers took the slightest notice of this. The white man, on his little bamboo stool, just managed to clear the tide! As the floods rose, we had to constantly dodge under the branches of the trees, while masses of long grass and tangled weed were cleared out of the way with a long stick. Here and there, fences were erected, leaving a gateway in the centre which formed a trap where fish were caught in abundance. You can imagine the problems of getting round these obstacles if your canoe missed the right route.

When the floods subsided, the mode of travel was by foot-slogging through slippery mud. Where stretches still lay under water, canoes might be available, but sometimes these were so narrow that it was a case of "standing room only", with loads skilfully balanced on the heads of the carriers. The slightest movement and all would have gone overboard. At other places we had to wade through deep water, one man going ahead with a long pole to make sure we did not disappear into a deep hole. Sometimes a tree-trunk bridge would begin ten feet from one bank and end thirty feet from the other. Here too, great care was needed to test the depth before stepping off. Later, when strong sun had baked the mud into rock-like ridges, the going was still tough, whether on foot or by bicycle, but in all our travelling we were conscious of the protecting hand of the God on whose business we were engaged.

The receding flood left rich soil which produced good crops and everyone worked hard on their farms, returning home after several days absence to eat, drink and make sacrifice. On one occasion I arrived at the village of Aike to discover a great crowd preparing to honour one of their idols. Among them were many young people, painted with different colours of clay and decorated with cowrie shell ornaments. Knowing what these orgies could be like, I felt thankful that my stay would be brief and sat down on one of my boxes to rest. Soon the headmen came to greet me,

"Are you staying with us tonight?" enquired their chief.

"No," I replied, "I'm moving ten miles farther on before dark."

"You must not go so soon," he protested. "If you stay there will be no revelry. I will call all the people to hear your word."

This suggestion amazed me, as many villages had gathered together for the ceremony, but what an opportunity – and what a meeting we had that evening! With the help of my boys, a tripod of bamboo sticks was erected for the lantern, which was operated by a pressure lamp. More bamboo poles were tied together to support the big white sheet which served as a screen. As the light of the moon glimmered through the trees, the town crier called out,

"Weke, weke!" (Be quiet!) and our meeting began.

It was too much to expect so many excited people to remain quiet throughout, so every few minutes I paused to allow them to respond in their own way. Then I blew a whistle, repeated,

"Weke!" and a hush fell upon the gathering once more.

The first slides showed some Igala Christians and their churches, which gave me a chance to tell of how the Gospel could change lives and communities. These were followed by pictures, illustrating the life and death of Christ. It moved me deeply to see the wonder on hundreds of up-turned faces as they heard about the Son of God who loved them and gave himself for them. The Holy Spirit was clearly at work, and when I returned to the village on my way home, four young men came to plead for someone to teach them more of God's word. No one was immediately available but I promised to answer their plea as soon as possible.

Two months later, while the Mission's General Secretary, Isaac McEwan, was with us at Idah, a deputation arrived to enquire if the teacher had yet been found. As we talked, one of the young men fumbled in the folds of his ragged garment and reached me £2.

"This is to help to pay for our teacher's support," he explained.

We were so impressed by the earnestness of these men that we felt their request must be given priority and before long they had their own teacher, church and school. Truly God had guided my footsteps to that village, from which, in the course of time, came one of our finest evangelists, Simon Onalo.

On the night of that memorable meeting one woman was absent. She had taken her baby daughter some miles away to a famous shrine at Odeke, in the hope of protection from the evil spirits whom she believed to be responsible for the deaths of several earlier children. Next day the people returned from Aike with wonderful stories about the white man's pictures and what he had taught them.

"He's coming here next," they said. "You'll hear him for yourself."

That was how Simon's mother first heard the name of Jesus, but she did not then become his follower. Her next child was a boy and at one year old he too became ill. The priest of the shrine was away at his farm so she laid her son on top of the idol, sure that he would be safe there. To her great shock the child died. She was too terrified to remove him herself and watched numbly while others lifted and buried the little limp body. Some days later she returned sorrowfully to her home, convinced that she would never have another child.

However, the time came when she realised that the idol had not only been powerless to save her child but was also unable to prevent her from conceiving again. Believers in her village had been telling her about the help other mothers had received from the white woman, so this time, instead of going to the shrine, she made her way up-river for her confinement. What rejoicing when she returned home again with a living, thriving child!

Now she began to attend Christian classes and tried to persuade her teen-age son to accompany her, but Simon was too busy carving idols to worship and to sell. Eventually he came with her to Idah dispensary and heard the Gospel clearly preached, but he didn't like the town and even the purchase of a new shirt could not coax him back for a while.

By the time the first teacher was installed at Odeke, Simon had decided that he wanted to go to school. He was encouraged by his mother but his father disapproved, so the lad sometimes slipped away from the family farm to attend reading classes. He formed a friendship with the teacher, who eventually persuaded the father to allow his son to accompany him to his home in Idah. There he learned to read and returned later with a little Scripture Gift Mission booklet entitled "The Way of Salvation", which he was able to read to the few believers in his village who were all illiterate.

At Unale the work of God was making good progress and Simon heard that a baptism class was being conducted there for those who wished to take a public stand as Christians. In spite of opposition, he walked the six miles every week, to attend this class and made a definite decision to trust the Lord Jesus as his Saviour. He was among the first to be baptised and soon afterwards his mother also committed herself to Christ.

Simon worked hard and gained entrance to the Mission school at Idah, hoping to join the police. His mother had promised the Lord her son would serve him for two years before taking up any other job and she was delighted when he decided to become a preacher. After serving in various towns, he went for further Bible training to Ilorin before being appointed District Evangelist with oversight of thirty-eight churches in Ibaji. He also received training as an officer in The Boys' Brigade and was used to form a number of companies in his own area. Simon was the greatest help to me during my time in Ibaji and it was good to see him and his wife again in 1978, in their present home in Idah.

The medical need of Ibaji was very great, partly due to the swampy conditions under which fierce mosquitos bred in abundance. During ten months in 1960-61, I reckoned to have treated about 8,000 patients and this pattern continued whenever I was available. Sometimes they came too late for help. One day after a preachers' class, I found a mother and grandmother waiting with a four-year-old boy. The child was moaning and almost unconscious, and I suspected that his bowel had been damaged by the strong native medicine often given in such cases. After doing what little I could for him, I left them to spend the night in the office which was next to my bedroom. At 1 a.m. all was quiet. Half an hour later the dispensary boy came to my window to say that the child was dead.

The grandmother was holding the precious little bundle as I tried to comfort them, talking of heaven and how we could meet our loved ones there. It was pouring with rain, but they wanted to go home right away. My helper took the dead child on his back and I covered them both with a plastic tablecloth. The grandmother got my raincoat. The mother put a cloth over her shoulders and carried a large basin on her head. A young man of their family carried their sleeping mats. I gave them a lantern and watched the sad procession set off through rain, mud and darkness on their two-mile journey. What a homecoming! Was it any wonder that I found it hard to think of leaving these people without even the limited medical help that I could offer?

Although there were sad cases, many had a happier ending – take Hannah and Rachel, for example. When my wife and I were in Idah, one of the motherless babies brought to us was a tiny girl from Ibaji and with the help of the church women we looked after her till she was old enough to return to her father. He was not a Christian and our only request was that she should not be forced into any pre-arranged heathen marriage.

After some years I was visiting Ibaji and was greeted by a tall figure on the river bank.

"Baba, do you not know me?" he asked.

At first I was baffled, but he went on,

"I am Rachel's father. Do you know I'm now a Christian? When I heard you were coming I prepared my house. Please come and stay with us tonight."

Well, it was thrilling to see Rachel again and to hear how her father had been led to the Saviour through the witness of a Christian from another village.

"We have no one here who can read," he told me. "I've been trying to learn so that we can have a service of our own but my reading is very hard for the people to follow. Could you send someone to stay and teach us the word of God properly?"

This was wonderful news. I asked if there were any other Christians in his village and was told,

"There is Hannah. Come and I'll take you to see her."

Hannah was at home in her tiny, windowless house. She was a middle-aged woman with a bright face. She had only one foot and hopped around with the aid of two short sticks. In answer to my enquiry she explained,

"I hurt my foot and it developed into an ulcer. None of our medicines could help. The ulcer ate into my leg until the bone rotted and I lost my foot."

As she talked, my eyes were becoming accustomed to the darkness inside the house and I noticed a small bundle on the mud platform which served as a bed. As I looked, the bundle stirred.

"Hannah," I asked, "is that a child?"

"Yes," she replied sadly, "that is my grand-daughter. Her mother died and we have no milk. For weeks she has had nothing but sugar and water. What more can we do?"

Even in the dim light I could see that the poor little mite looked more like a skeleton than a living child. Something must be done at once if she was not to die.

"Where is the child's father?" I asked. "He must come with me and I will give him milk and cod liver oil and medicines to last for a month. Then he can come back for another supply."

Nine years later Hannah heard that I was holding a clinic two miles away from her home. She walked there to see me, using the good crutches I had been able to send her, and with her came her lovely nine-year-old granddaughter – another Rachel. Hannah returned three times that week for treatment for a skin disease, and as she waited she told her story to the women around her, full of praise to God for his goodness. Isn't it a privilege to show such people something of his kindness?

Independence came to Nigeria on 1st October, 1960, and great celebrations took place throughout the land. That day I was visiting the Ibaji village of Uchuchu and as I passed the school on my way to find a lodging place the children were lined up to begin their sports. Suddenly the headmaster came hurrying towards me.

"Please sir," he said, "would you be willing to address the school on this special occasion?"

"Certainly," I replied. "It will be a pleasure to do so."

There was no time for preparation so he introduced

me immediately to the assembled company, saying,

"We are very privileged to be the only village in Ibaji to have a white man to address us at our Independence celebration."

My remarks, on the spur of the moment, were based on the thought of Freedom – freedom to rule their own country and freedom from the rule of sin. After the speeches I sat with village leaders to watch the sports, and took the opportunity to invite them to attend our service the next day. They all came and listened with interest. As a result there has been a church and a preacher in that village ever since – just another example of how God overrules, and often interrupts, our programme for the fulfilment of his purposes.

The Ibajis loved a celebration so we always tried to make the Christian festivals a time of fellowship and rejoicing. Christmas 1970 stands out in my mind because the boxes with my supply of little gifts was held up at Lagos and the prizes for Boxing Day sports consisted of a few pence, or whatever items of clothing or household goods could possibly be spared. I had been longing for a piece of fresh meat for a change from the tinned variety, but all my efforts were in vain. I had reconciled myself to "no special fare" when a boy arrived with a big crate on his head. He was a student at our secondary school at Ochaja and as he set down his load he said,

"This is for you from our Principal."

Can you believe it? When I opened the crate what did I see but a lovely big turkey! Thanks to the thoughtfulness of my Igala "son", Daniel Enfola, and the loving provision of my heavenly Father, we had a wonderful Christmas dinner. As I wrote home, afterwards,

"Who wouldn't be a missionary?"!

The sufferings of the Ibaji people during the civil war have been mentioned in the previous chapter, but the after-effects continued to be felt for a considerable time. Everywhere I went, there were burned-out houses, devastated farms and under-nourished people. Idol houses had not escaped the general destruction and for a time it seemed as if the grip of spirit-worship might be loosening. Nearly every Sunday someone was standing up in church as a sign of repentance and desire to follow Christ.

One day when I was preaching in a village about four miles away, a man's name was read out as having repented and he was asked to stand. He was an elderly man, father of the local headmaster, and there, in the middle of the congregation of about five hundred people, he leaped up, threw his hands above his head and cried out,

"I've come!"

"Thanks be to God," responded the worshippers.

After the service I visited the preacher's father, who was the head pagan priest of that town. He was just leaving his idol house and seemed glad to see me. We chatted for a while, then I told him about the man in church and asked,

"When will you be coming?"

"I'll be coming," he assured me with a smile, but I am still waiting to hear that he has kept his promise.

Of all the burdens on my heart, none lay heavier than that for the old men of Ibaji. We were good friends, able to talk freely together, and often they would say,

"If we had heard this message when we were young, we would have repented. Now we are too old to change from the way of our fathers."

Even though their sacred things had proved powerless against the invaders, they soon replaced them with new ju-ju, rebuilding the idol houses alongside their own dwellings. But there was one noticeable change. They no longer so fiercely opposed their sons who wanted a better way of life, and a number of them were proving their ability in our secondary school at Ochaja.

After the civil war, the Christian Council in Nigeria sent a representative to investigate the medical needs of the area and, as a result of his report, a grant was made for the erection of a Health Centre at Enweli. Building again proved to be a long and difficult job, but by 1976 the centre was in operation under the guidance of Ibaji's first doctor, Derek Belgrave, who now has the help of his wife, a qualified and capable nurse.

I have vivid recollections of my final term of service in Ibaji when I relieved Dr. Belgrave for a short time after returning from furlough in 1973. While I was at home the bulldozers had begun work on the new road and Norman Dack, who was then missionary at Idah, was able to take me the first twelve miles by pick-up. At that point six carriers were waiting with bicycles, one of them ready to carry me on the crossbar. I had already experienced this undignified form of travel and was prepared for the worst. It was necessary to keep my feet stretched out to clear the pedals and after about a mile one leg decided to go to sleep, so I had to dismount and walk a bit. This process was repeated for nine miles, but for the last four miles the going was too rough for the cycles and everyone had to walk. What did you say? Yes, of course I was stiff and sore. But who wouldn't be, at 79 years of age?

My first engagement was to conduct a service to commission three corporals for a new company of The Boys' Brigade. The church was packed, and this in a town where there had been little evidence of spiritual interest. Boys were crowding into all of the eight Ibaji companies under the enthusiastic leadership of Evangelist Simon Onalo, and, at the end of September that year, many of them travelled to Idah to take part in Nigeria's thirteenth Independence Day celebrations. To get there, two hundred and forty-seven boys, plus officers, walked through mud and water from their flooded villages. Some who passed Enweli on their way, walked fourteen miles one day and twenty on the next, many of them never having been far from home before, or seen a car or lorry. Rather than leave the small boys behind, the bigger ones had decided to carry them when they got tired, and so all arrived safely for the great event.

They were warmly received by the Idah church people and accommodated in the school compound. On Sunday morning they made a fine procession, marching two abreast in lovely clean uniforms to the church service. In the afternoon they had Sunday School in the shade of the big trees and, as they studied John 3:16, many boys confessed wrong-doing and were led to trust the Lord as their personal Saviour. One lad who had been turned out of his pagan home for going to church, testified that he was now a Christian and was praying for his parents.

Monday was the big day, and they were joined by some other Boys' and Girls' Brigade members to parade through the town with bands and placards on which had been written verses from the Igala Bible. One policeman, reading a placard, was heard to say in wonderment,

"What! Jesus Christ died for me? I must look into this!"

The Government had arranged a football match for that afternoon and the Ibaji boys were asked to give a display on the ground at half-time. At the end of the game they were asked for a final item and once again, with the great crowd surrounding the field, the boys gave of their best and were cheered to the echo. What stories they had to tell when they reached home, and what a wonderful witness they left behind, among Christians, Muslims and pagans alike!

I had been asked to open up new work across the Niger, so I knew that my time in Ibaji was drawing to a close. The first school had just been started at Enweli under the Native Authority. Its pupils were all boys, mostly from pagan homes, and I was concerned that none of them were attending church. After praying for guidance, I asked the headmaster if he would allow me to tell them how the Gospel and education had come to their villages. He readily agreed and they were all very interested. Then I went on to tell about the translation of the Scriptures into their own language and the great reception given to the first complete Bibles which had arrived at Idah in 1971.

"How many boys have a copy of this word of God?" I asked.

Only one hand went up, and, without further comment, I promised,

"Any boy who begins from now and attends church until Christmas will received an Igala Bible of his very own."

The following Sunday, fifteen boys were at the service and had their names recorded in an exercise book. A week later four more were added. When there were forty-one on the list, I decided to call a halt, but it was grand to see the Scriptures in the hands of these lads and to know that they would be able to read them for themselves and their families. Today there is not only a primary school but also a secondary school in Enweli. How important it was for these promising young people to learn that the fear of the Lord is the beginning of wisdom.

On the first Sunday of 1979 I preached to a congregation of over six hundred in the big new church at Unale and, looking over the reverent gathering of young and old, I thought to myself, "What a change from our early visits to this stronghold of the devil."

After the service James Odekwe came forward with a fine little boy of eight years old, accompanied by his older brother.

"Do you remember Friday of Odolu?" he asked.

Friday – the motherless baby brought to me at three days old by his crippled father! How could I ever forget that forlorn little family, left without the one who had been both mother and breadwinner? She had been a Christian and named her older children Rachel, Gabriel and Godwin, but she had been too ill to choose a name for the baby so he was called for the day of his birth. I was able to get a supply of Ostermilk and an old Christian woman to care for the infant. Through the kindness of friends at home, Gabriel's school fees had been paid and other help given as necessary.

Two years later the father died, having also come to know the Lord. Rachel looked after her brothers faithfully and is now married, with two children of her own. Five days after I saw her brothers, she sought me out at Enweli, having walked many miles with the baby and her husband, who is the evangelist in their village. It was as good as a tonic to see them all so well and happy in God's service.

During my stay with James Odekwe an old friend came and sat beside me on the verandah. He spoke with pride about his Christian son, who had helped me in the dispensary and later joined the Nigerian police. Then he went on to praise the improvements in Ibaji and the progress of their people, attributing some of these changes to my work over the years. When he paused, I said quietly,

"Father, when I came to Ibaji, you and all the old men were pleased about the medical help but did not want the word of God or schools. For years you held these up."

He hung his head for a moment, then looked up and said simply,

"It is true, but I'm very glad our opposition did not turn you back."

Is it really too late for this dear man and others like him, to turn from their idols to serve the living and true God?

CHAPTER THIRTEEN

The Second Watch

It was one thing to have arrived in Ibaji by car, but quite another to get out again! However, my transport problem was solved by the unexpected appearance at the Health Centre of an Assistant Superintendent of Police. After consulting the doctor, he agreed to take me back with him by car to Unale, where, to her surprise, I met his wife, Rhoda, another of the girls brought up by us at Idah! He kindly arranged for the driver of a small van to take me the rest of the way, in time to catch the ferry across the river to Bendel State – the scene of my final, and in some ways most difficult, term of service in Nigeria.

Our interest in Bendel State had been aroused by a missionary engaged in the New Life For All movement, who reported that, although several churches were working in the area, there was no Bible-based evangelical witness. He suggested that the Qua Iboe Mission might consider it as a possible new field. At that time we could not see our way to take on further responsibility but kept the matter before the Lord in prayer.

When Dr. Belgrave was appointed to Ibaji, I was invited to pioneer the new work, and on 14th November 1973 made my first trip across the Niger, accompanied by Pastor Joseph Okpanachi and missionary Norman Dack. The ferry was not working so we crossed by canoe and an hour later began our walk to the chief's palace, where his Highness, the

Oba of the district, gave us a very cordial welcome. We had a letter of introduction from the postmaster of Idah, who was a native of that part, but the Oba himself already knew the Qua Iboe Mission as he had been an Inspector of Police in Calabar Province.

At the close of our interview we arranged another visit, and he promised an escort and letter of introduction to places which had been suggested as possible headquarters. A week later we returned and began this new venture by visiting the chiefs and people of three centres, and asking many questions about the water supply, medical needs and religious groups in the vicinity. Eventually we decided to give priority to a place called Agiere, about eleven miles from the larger town of Agenebode. Remarkably, Agiere had a dispensary building, erected many years before by their district council and completed by the community but never used, as there was no one to staff it. It had no furniture or equipment but seemed otherwise very suitable for our work.

The postmaster, who was a Roman Catholic, told us that many baptised members had left that church to become Muslims. There was also a group called the Seraphim-Cherubim, but nothing of the Scriptures had been translated into Etsako, the language of the Weppa Wanno people. Two permanent military camps were within easy reach, and a number of schools, but there was no youth work, such as Boys' Brigade. God had clearly led us to a centre with great possibilities for his Kingdom.

When the time came to move in, I was given a great welcome by the Administration Department of the Government and other officials. They were delighted at the prospect of their dispensary being opened at last and expressed their approval by signing the visitors' book. From that time on, between eighty and a hundred patients turned up for treatment every week day and the atmosphere was most friendly. My chief problem was lack of trained helpers, as my cook from Ibaji was the only one who even knew what a tablet was, but I was anxious to employ local people as soon as possible.

In my dwelling house things were a bit rough, but accommodation was sufficient and it was just across the road from the dispensary. There was no ceiling to keep the dust from the roof and crumbling walls from falling on everything, so I found some big pieces of boarding and fastened them across the beams. After that we felt better prepared for the strong winds of harmattan. It seemed strange to be in a town, with the main road about forty feet from the door and taxis flying past at sixty miles an hour. At night, when traffic eased off, the noise level was maintained by radios at full blast and beer drinking parties – all very different from the swamps of Ibaji.

Being unable to speak the language reminded me of early days in other places, but a young man agreed to interpret in the services and quickly showed interest in the Christian message. The first Sunday there were only my two boys in the audience, but the following Sunday we had four, and the third week brought more than forty. It was interesting to see many of the folk crossing themselves as they entered. As well as having no Scripture in Etsako, we also missed having any hymns to sing but, all in all, I felt encouraged by the start that had been made.

During those first six busy weeks I treated 1,700 patients and received several requests to open other clinics. Then the sudden blow fell which changed everything. A young African doctor, in government service 22 miles away, arrived with members of his staff and a policeman. He challenged my authority to operate a dispensary and ordered me to pack all medicines for removal. My efforts to explain went unheeded and he insisted that I must make a statement at the police station at Auchi. This I agreed to do, as soon as I had reported the whole affair to the Oba who had authorised and encouraged my work.

All this happened in the middle of a busy dispensary and, when the remaining patients realised that there would be no more treatment, trouble began. By the time I returned from the Oba, the villagers had rioted. Two of the doctor's assistants, seen carrying off the medicines, had been beaten up and his car put out of action. Reinforcements of police had arrived and used tear gas to disperse the crowd. My helpers and I were arrested and taken before the Commissioner of Police. After making a full statement I was brought back to Agiere, but my poor boys were detained because they had been there during the riot.

"When will I be wanted again?" I asked, and was told,

"If we want you we will come for you."

That was the beginning of a long wait for a court case which never came. I later learned that the trouble had really arisen between two government departments, one of which had authorised my occupancy without consulting the other, and my position could easily have been resolved if the people had not rioted. All this was unknown to me as I looked across at the closed dispensary and resisted the pleas of patients needing medicine. Was this the work of the enemy of souls, or was it God's way of directing me to another sphere of service?

On the morning after the riot, having committed the whole situation to the Lord, I waited on him to know what my next step should be. There, in the early quietness, he flashed into my mind the thought,

"These people have nothing of my word in their own tongue."

"True, Lord," I responded. "Is this the work you have planned for me?"

The more I considered it, the surer I felt of his call to the task of translation. But how should I go about it, knowing nothing of the language? First of all I enquired if there was anyone engaged in Christian work with whom I could co-operate, and was told of an Apostolic pastor at Agenebode. When we met I realised that he was a spiritual person, and when translation of the Bible was mentioned he responded with enthusiasm,

"I have longed for this for years but never felt able to do it. I will gladly help in any way I can."

So, at almost eighty years of age, I was privileged to begin the translation of God's precious word into yet another tongue!

Perhaps the atmosphere of this period can best be conveyed by quoting from letters written to friends at home who were standing with me in prayer.

April 1974.

"Even though the dispensary is closed people still keep coming every day. God has certainly used the treatments and I have urged those concerned to thank him. Meanwhile we await a settlement fo the court case and until then the dispensary must remain closed. The boys have been released from prison, but the date of the case has been postponed till the end of May. Very many people have come to see me and I have had interesting talks. One young man who knew us years ago in Idah, introduced himself as a born-again Christian! He lives just 11 miles away and plans to come to our Sunday services."

May 1974.

"I have just got back from the service where fifty-six, including children, were present. I have begun on the Ten Commandments. Last Sunday we had our first English service with an audience of six, and I am hoping others will soon join us."

Next day – "I have been out from 9 a.m. till 6 p.m. and have visited eight villages. The Agiere 'doctor's' fame was known everywhere and people were very friendly. Of course I was asked to hold clinics but that will be decided later. These days have not been lost. God will work out his plan for these people and will show us as a mission the part we are to play in it."

August 1974.

"I may be preparing the atmosphere for those who follow and I am not worrying about whether or not I am allowed to do medical work. I am busy with the translation of Scripture Gift Mission booklets and with the people around me."

September 1974.

"The translation of 'The Way of Salvation' has had a set-back. Mr. Odjor, who was helping me, died suddenly last Saturday. On Tuesday I went to see the family and met another pastor of the Apostolic Church who was to join the translation group. He seems a good man and I will arrange with him to go on with this work. The S.G.M. have written to say they prefer to begin with the booklets, 'Come' and 'Listen' so we will do these first."

"Salihu, my interpreter, has learned to type and is now teaching seven other boys. He reached fifty words a minute in his last test and will be a great help in the translation. These other boys were at a loose end and it brings them under Christian influence. They will easily get work with a knowledge of typing. Each one has been given an S.G.M. booklet to read.

At the end of the week we read it together and I question them to see if they understand it. That is their English lesson!

"Our Sunday evening service is more like a Bible Study Class for those who can read English. Up to date around nine come. We have choruses, then read the portion with everyone sharing. I correct the pronunciation, explain the meaning of words, and then teach the passage, verse by verse. Today after the service two young boys asked for Bibles. So, amid what could be frustration, God is encouraging us."

October 1974.

"As I set outside my house after dark I know something of the second Beatitude, and as I see the sin and darkness around me I can only pray – 'Lord, I am helpless. You alone can change these people, and surely you must do it, for are they not included in your love and salvation, shown forth at Calvary?' Then I take comfort in the assurance that they are precious in his sight. He has a plan which will not fail to be fulfilled."

"Translation goes on slowly as those I require for checking have their own work and can only come at certain times. These last eight months have called for endurance but we still go on and are not cast down. I am seldom without African visitors, and the Lord has so helped me in this situation that I am very happy and in good health."

December 1974.

"My main reason for this letter is to say that we have sent the first portion of the Bible ever translated into Etsako to the S.G.M. in London. It is the booklet 'Come' and has the Christmas story in it. Last Sunday we read John 3:16 in Etsako and got the people to repeat it. I sent typewritten copies to various churches so, for the first time, people will hear the Christmas story in their own language. We will now go on with 'Listen' and 'The Way of Salvation'."

January 1975.

"It is wonderful how loyal many people are in their prayer support and I never needed it more than during this tour. The court case has been adjourned once more, this time until March 24th. It would seem as if the magistrate and lawyers want to wear us out, and this may go on until I leave for home in May. The translation work goes on and I hope soon to send the second manuscript to London. It is now 11 a.m. and this has been a very hard morning. Many sick folk won't believe that I'm not allowed to do clinics and twice I've had to close my door and go for a walk to convince them that I cannot attend them. With a store full of useful drugs it is miserable to send them away."

During that difficult time of house arrest with no charge brought against me, I often felt like hiring a lawyer and bringing my own case to court. Many government officials were willing to back me and the Oba himself had said,

"If you bring a case to law, I will be your first witness."

The administrator agreed that I was in a good position but when I felt this wrong attitude of resentment rising within me, the Lord graciously blew a nice cooling breath over my hot spirit, saying,

"The servant of the Lord must not strive; but be gentle unto all men . . . . patient . . . . in meekness instructing those that oppose themselves."

"Thank you, Lord," my heart replied, "You are right. Keep me always honouring and trusting you."

One day I had a visit from a man who had received

medical help for himself and his family, and was very upset by the closure of this work. I gave him the English version of John 3:16 and, when he had read it, I handed him the typewritten translation of the same verse. I watched his lips moving as he quietly read the words. Suddenly his face lit up and he burst out,

"This is my language!"

"Yes," I said, "and we hope to translate the whole Bible."

With that he exclaimed, almost shouting with excitement,

"I'm glad your dispensary has been stopped for now we will have the word of God in our own tongue!"

Truly God's thoughts are not our thoughts, nor our ways his ways. One voice was silenced in the dispensary but thousands more were to be released through his written word.

In this middle of this trying period it was refreshing to join with fellow-missionaries for the quarterly prayer day at Ochadamu on 12th October. I had been asked to speak at the morning session and my message was not so much a sermon as a warning, a comfort and an encouragement from God, based on Luke 12:33-40, and especially verse 28 – *"and if he shall come in the second watch."*

These words had come to me when praying about the meeting and so stuck in my mind that I felt they were given for myself, going through a "second watch" experience just then, and to pass on to others who must face similar times when loyalty to Christ would be tested. Speaking very personally, but I hope gently, I referred to experiences in the lives of David Livingstone, Mackay of Uganda and J.G. Paton, who found, in the severest test, that the Lord Jesus was with them according to his promise, bringing them through into the "morning watch" of glorious victory, as in Exodus 14:24 ff and John 21:4 ff. God spoke to us all that morning. But there was more to come – in a very different vein!

One of the lovely things about a mission like ours is the mutual caring which transforms colleagues into a family. Perhaps I have been especially blessed in having my wife's two nieces and one grand-niece as fellow-missionaries for longer or shorter periods, and, at this particular time, our grand-niece, Elizabeth, was in Igala with her husband, John Ross, and their two little children. I was congratulating myself that no-one had remembered my 80th birthday, when, just before the evening meal, an announcement was made that somebody was soon coming of age! There was no use trying to deny it for some of the folks had seen my passport, their only doubt being as to the exact date. The cat was out of the bag, so I had to admit that 15th was indeed my special day.

"Happy Birthday to you," sang out everybody, the ladies produced a beautiful cake with a large *"80"* iced on top, and one of them held my hand while I cut it. After everyone had enjoyed a piece, I thought to myself, "Well, that's over," and settled down to nurse my great-grand-nephew. Before long, however, the baby was lifted from my arms and I was propelled to the front of the house, where the company had assembled to sing "Happy Birthday" again and present me with a card from "The Family" and a big round basket, full of all sorts of provisions to take back with me to Agiere the next day. Then John Ross committed us to the Lord in prayer and we all sang the doxology.

That wasn't the first time Ochadamu had been the setting for a surprise party. Two years previously, at the Prayer Day on 3rd June 1972, another wonderful cake appeared, saved by one young missionary from Christmas, and iced by another with white and yellow icing. On it was a crown and the words *"50 years in Royal Service"*. But that was not all, for my dear friends had joined together to present me with a lovely watch, to mark the fiftieth anniversary of my arrival in Nigeria. Can you wonder that I repeat, again and again, "Who wouldn't be a missionary?"!

Time for furlough was drawing near and I had to consider the future. My sister was needing to be cared for at home and I was now in my eighties, so a further term of service in Nigeria seemed unlikely. However, I hoped to at least return for a visit, and decided to keep the door open by obtaining a re-entry permit. The bigger problem was, who would continue the work in Bendel State? I was praying that the Qua Iboe Church across the river would be given the missionary vision and courage to accept the challenge, and that God would call the man of his choice to take my place. Meanwhile, who would conduct the services? My thoughts were directed to Simon Onalo from Ibaji, who had recently been appointed Youth Organiser and was now living in Idah. He agreed to come over as regularly as possible, but could not promise every Sunday.

Many children had crowded to my house when I first arrived at Agiere. As the days passed, curiosity waned and the numbers decreased, but two school boys kept coming in the evenings, keen to improve their English and get help with their lessons. One of them had an unusual name. He had been born a week before Nigeria gained independence, so he was called Independent. He came from a Muslim home and lived nearby with his mother, while his father, in another part of the town, took no interest in him.

It soon became evident that this boy was very interested in God's word, asking many questions and attending all our services. His joy was great when he realised that Jesus had died for his sins, and before long he trusted him as his Saviour. From the English Bible which I had given him and from our talks together, he learned about the second coming of our Lord and began to encourage other people to get ready for that great event.

When the day came for me to leave Agiere it was a sad parting, as there was no human helper to take over. In such a situation one must trust without seeing, assured that the God who led us to this place had his own plans for continuing his work. Beside me, as I said goodbye, stood this lad, now fourteen years of age, who in later months had been helping me in the house and meetings.

"Independent," I said, trying to cheer him up, "If no one comes from Igala to conduct the service next Sunday, you must be the one to do it."

He looked surprised but did not reply. Soon after reaching home I received a letter which read,

"...that Sunday you referred to, it happened as you said. No-one came from Igala and I had to take the service. We sang all the hymns and choruses we have (8 hymns and 10 choruses) then I preached from Luke 17:1–21 and closed by asking a man to pray. The following Sunday the Igala evangelist came, a very kind man, and more people came to the service than when you were here."

Well, no one is indispensable! Simon Onalo continued to go to Agiere when he could, but this provided no long-term solution to the problem and much earnest prayer was made for a missionary – whether Nigerian or ex-patriate. Back at our old station at Adoru, our wonderful God was preparing his answer.

John Akogwu had been one of my students at Ankpa Bible School, where he was familiarly known as "Congo". He was one of our best footballers and a faithful, hard-working student. After completing the course he went on to our Bible College at Abak, returning three years later to be appointed evangelist at Adoru. John had followed with interest the opening of work in Bendel State and knew of the need for someone to take my place. What a happy surprise it was to learn that this good man had heard God's call to go there, and that his offer had been accepted by the Qua Iboe Church!

It was not easy for John and his wife to face up to moving across the Niger with their five children, to live in a noisy, sinful town, among people of a different tongue, but God gave the needed grace and blessed their witness. Soon there were three preaching centres and so many opportunities for further outreach that John, who did not enjoy the best of health, could not tackle them all by himself. He began to pray for a fellow-worker. Indeed his concern was so great that he shared it with one of the tutors at Abak, and sent a generous portion of his "tithe" to help pay for the training of whoever God might call to join him in the missionary task.

Once again, the Lord of the harvest had been anticipating the prayer for labourers. Away down in Qua Iboe country, a young preacher who had completed one year's preliminary training at the Bible College was strangely disturbed by a recurring call in his heart, "Northern Nigeria, northern Nigeria." He could not understand this, but shared it with his wife and together they prayed for guidance. Before the year was out he was sure that God was calling him to serve outside his immediate neighbourhood, and decided to enroll for the two-year diploma course in the Bible College for 1977-78.

The thought of northern Nigeria receded during the first year but came back with renewed force early in 1978. In the providence of God, this student, David Udoudem, was chosen with two others to go to Bendel State for a week's evangelistic trek that April. Under the guidance of John Akogwu, they visited seventeen villages, conducted many meetings and spoke to numbers of pagan, Muslim and Roman Catholic people. They were deeply impressed by the need and, as they joined in prayer before leaving, David was moved to tears, though he did not fully understand the reason. One thing was puzzling him, and it was a matter of geography. Surely Bendel State was in western, not northern Nigeria?

At the end of term a letter from John Akogwu was read aloud by the college Principal.

"Come over to Macedonia, that is to say, cross the Niger and help us," was its appeal.

David Udoudem was convinced. Bendel might be in the mid-west, but it was certainly 400 miles north of where he now lived. With the loyal backing of his wife, he offered himself for service there and within a few months had moved, with his four children, to join the Akogwus as pioneer evangelists of the Qua Iboe Church.

At the same time, the translation was being carried forward by the Apostolic pastors, who kept in close touch by correspondence with me in Scotland. The first Scripture Gift Mission booklet in Etsako had reached Nigeria in December 1976, and Pastor Asemokai wrote about its reception,

"The enthusiasm was marvellous and the first packets were used up right away. An old man of seventy years was so delighted that he said he must come to the reading class so that he could learn to read it for himself. His Highness, the Oba, was so delighted as he heard it read that he said he must record his gratitude to Mr. Dickson on a cassette to be sent to him. He hoped that such good work would go on, and that a committee should be formed to take up this translation."

The Information Office at Auchi received a copy of "Vhare", which is the Etsako word for "Come", and were so pleased to have something in their own language that they decided to use it as the primer for literacy classes in their division. So the word of God was being sown ever more widely. And more packets of the precious seed were in preparation!

When the opportunity came to revisit Nigeria, I made up my mind that most of my time must be spent in Bendel State as I was keen to see the progress of the work and to give encouragement and help where needed. David Udoudem was now living at Agiere but John Akogwu had moved to Agenebode, the largest town in the Weppa Wanno clan. He met me with a taxi at the ferry on Monday 15th January 1979, and took me to his home where I was to spend the following six weeks. It was good to be with him again!

John and David had worked hard. They now had the care of ten little church groups and were preparing twelve believers for the first baptismal service, to be held later that year. Wherever I went people greeted me warmly, remembering the "doctor" of Agiere and often bringing gifts of eggs or other food in gratitude for help given during my short time in the dispensary. Independent was no longer in that area but my typist, Salihu, having done well at commercial college in Idah, was now a boarder in the grammar school at Agenebode and able to help some of the newly-planted churches at weekends.

This was the hottest time of the year and it was hard to sleep in a bath of perspiration. Thieves were on the prowl and windows had to be made secure, but my good friends did all they could for my comfort. Two days after my arrival I had a pleasant surprise when Pastor Asemokai arrived with a portable fan which provided a most welcome breeze when the electricity was on, every other evening.

Most of my days were spent in checking the translation which had been done by him and Mr. Anaemhomhe, who had joined him in the work. This new helper was obviously gifted by God and had already made a start on the Gospels, Acts, Romans and Corinthians. Our immediate objective was to prepare the Gospel of Mark for submission to the Bible Translators' Society in Jos, and we managed to get this completed by the 26th January. After thorough testing among Etsako-speaking people, the society approved our manuscript and sent it on for printing by the International Bible Society of New York. I was able to arrange for our two translators to attend a special course in Jos, before tackling their next book – the Gospel according to John.

So, with several S.G.M. booklets in the hands of the people; with the first book of the New Testament in the hands of a Bible Society; with the continuing work of translation and church-planting in the hands of good men, and committing all into the hand of God, I took my leave of Bendel State on 22nd February. How true it is that *"all things work together for good to those who love God"* – if only we have the wisdom and patience to leave the over-ruling to him!

CHAPTER FOURTEEN

Manifold More

In our early days of trekking through the long grass, forest and swamp of Igala and Ibaji, I could never have imagined that one day I would preach to people from these areas in big Qua Iboe churches in the crowded cities of modern Nigeria. Yet this tranformation has taken place within my own lifetime. How did it happen?

As the new generation of educated young people arose, they found few job opportunities in their own villages and many of them set out to seek employment in the townships. They brought their own form of worship with them and began to hold services in their homes, using the Igala or Efik Bibles and hymnbooks with which they were well acquainted. Many of them prospered and invited others to come where there was work, and friends who spoke the same language. From these beginnings, the house groups grew into congregations which, in turn, built churches to accommodate hundreds, and in some cases thousands of worshippers.

The first township church that I visited in October 1978, however, was not an Igala congregation in the north, but one which had sprung up in similar fashion in the historic southern port of Calabar. Many a time, in days gone by, I had travelled there by river. Now, the improved road system enabled Pastor Amos Udonsak to take me direct by car from the Bible College at Abak, arriving in good time for the Qua

Iboe Church's anniversary service at 10 a.m.

How am I to describe that service? The well-built church had electric light, fans and amplifiers, reaching to all sections of the thousand-strong congregation. A great platform accommodated about forty members of the choir on my right and on either side of the reading desk seven elders were seated, facing inwards. I sat behind the desk, between Pastor Udonsak and Pastor Umoren, who has done so much to build up the Qua Iboe Church in Calabar.

By the time the introductory remarks were over, I began to wonder who they were talking about and how I would face this great assembly, but I was on the Lord's business and he helped me to deliver the message for that day on "The rôle of Christians in the world."

After the benediction, I was breathing a sigh of relief when up came a young man with a microphone, and another who began to read an address of welcome. Then the chairman of the Women's Fellowship presented me with a beautifully carved ebony fish, to remind me that, although there were plenty of fish in the Qua Iboe river, I, like our Mission's founder, Samuel Bill, had followed the Lord and become a "fisher of men". Later I found that the parcel also contained a generous gift of money – their thank-offering for the coming of the Gospel which has done so much for Nigerian womanhood.

As we left the platform, I was surrounded by crowds of people whose parents had known me in early days, before being dragged away to the hall for light refreshments and the cutting of a beautiful cake, iced with the words:

"WELCOME TO REV. H.W. DICKSON."

When will it end? While eating, I was told that the

Press was waiting for an interview and for nearly an hour I was kept answering questions and recalling conditions in Nigeria in bygone days, the final splendid question being –

"What advice would you give to the youth of today?"

"God has a plan for your life too," was my reply. "Accept the Lord Jesus as your Saviour and he will open it up for you as is promised in Psalm 32 verse 8 – *'I will instruct thee and teach thee in the way which thou shalt go: I will guide thee with mine eye'*."

Tired but happy, I recorded in my diary that night, "The whole visit was a wonderful occasion and unforgettable to me."

A full page report and photograph of this interview appeared in the Nigerian Chronicle. It began,

"Far into the womb of time past – by a long span of 56 years – is the year 1922. In that year, on August 4, an ocean liner from Liverpool, SS Elmina, steamed to berth in Calabar. From it a young European from Port Glasgow walked out, with a Bible in his luggage . . . and 56 years after, on Sunday, October 22, Rev. Dickson showed up again in Calabar, wearing 84 years of age and glad to have braved the odds to undertake missionary work in Nigeria."

How right that young reporter was in his assessment!

The following Sunday we set out again for another anniversary service, this time in Port Harcourt, a town of growing size and importance because of its big oil refinery. There are three flourishing Qua Iboe churches in "P.H.", and as many more in the sprawling suburbs. The plan was that I should preach at one church and make a brief call at a couple of others, but it did not work out that way. Pastor Udonsak and I got a rousing welcome at the first church while other members of the Bible College team went on to different congregations. As our service closed, a car drew up at the rear door and two men came in and spoke to the pastor. He looked anxiously at me and I enquired,

"What's up now?"

"These men are from the church two miles away in the town centre," he said. "They say their people won't go home until they hear the old missionary!"

Well, it warms the heart of any old missionary to be wanted by the people he loves. What could I do but agree to go? And what excitement when we arrived with that congregation of seven hundred waiting people!

After the usual introduction and remarks about my great age, I felt something must be done to relieve the tension, so, speaking in their own Efik language, I said,

"All that the principal has said is true. Sometimes my legs say to me, 'You are getting old,' but then my heart replies, 'It is not so, I am still a young man'."

At that the congregation broke into loud applause and when they eventually settled down the tension was gone. Many of them were young people and I challenged them with the claims of Christ and their responsibility for carrying on his work in the future. Afterwards they crowded round with a photographer to have a picture taken with me in their midst.

On we went to the third church, with poor Pastor Udonsak apologising for my having to preach three sermons instead of one! After a sumptuous lunch we drove back to the Bible College, humbled by the love of these dear Christian people. That evening we enjoyed a time of fellowship with college staff and students, and were much moved to hear the Principal's testimony, based on Psalm 103:4, *"Who redeemeth thy life from destruction."* He told how, because of something unusual at his birth, his life and that of his mother were threatened. God, in his goodness, had protected and spared them for the fulfilment of his own purposes – for that little child was destined to become the first Nigerian Principal of the Q.I.C. Bible College.

A month later I spent five days with the Qua Iboe Church in Makurdi, the State capital on the river Benue, north-east of Igala. My escort during this visit was to be Elder Abel Adaji, until now only slightly known to me, though we had met many years before. As we went from place to place he told me his story.

Abel came from a village some miles behind Gwalawo, through which I had trekked in the 1930's. One day, as a small boy, he was running around with the other children when his father dashed out in great excitement. He rushed all the children into the house, pushed them into an inner room, closed the door and warned them not to speak or make any noise.

"There's a strange thing coming along the bush path towards the house," he said. "It must be from the devil because it's coming very fast and it has no legs!"

He shut the outside door and watched through a crack in the wood, while the children peered through a chink in the inner door to see what would happen. Why all the excitement?

"Baba," Abel explained, "this was your first visit to our village. You came by bicycle and we had never seen one before! After you passed through we learned that no one had been harmed and that you had spoken kindly to the people. Later on you sent one of the Igala Christians to live in our village. He began to teach the children to read and held services to tell us about God's love and salvation. After some years my father and mother and all our family became Christians and there has been an encouraging witness there ever since."

Today, Abel is one of the heads of the government printing department at Makurdi, and a respected elder, playing an active part in building up the Qua Iboe church with its congregation of many hundreds. Although the Tiv tribe occupy this area, there are a good many Igalas in government positions and Abel told me that five of them who knew me when they were young, had asked him to take me to visit them. So, when the Sunday morning and afternoon services were over, we set out on our rounds at 4 p.m.

The first call was at the house of the Secretary to the Military Government, where we had coffee while we talked; then on to the Permanent Secretary to the Ministry of Health. I cannot recall the position of number three but he was a very spiritually-minded man who had been brought up by Mr. Gross of the C.M.M.L. Our next call was at the home of a High Court judge, whose wife I have known since birth as she was the daughter of the late Peter Achimugu. After a loving welcome, their little four-year-old girl climbed on to my knee and sat contentedly there as we talked together about many things. Then, when the time came to part, the father drew his four children around him and stood beside me, while Elizabeth knelt and I committed them all to God in prayer.

"Where are you going after you leave Makurdi?" enquired the judge.

"Back to Ochadamu," I replied.

"But that is 170 miles away," he said. "How are you travelling?"

"I hope to get a taxi."

"A taxi!" he exclaimed, "When I have a car with a driver! They will call for you at 8 a.m. tomorrow morning."

My last visit that Sunday was to the Commissioner of Finance, Paul Achimugu, another child of my good friend. He is an elder of the church, most highly respected, and on the University Board for Benue State. My escort and I had supper at his home – a lovely ending to a great day! Next morning, true to the judge's word, a chauffeur-driven car arrived at the pastor's house where I was staying. Elizabeth thought that every old person needed conversation on a journey, so my host, Maurice Idoko, a former student of Ankpa and Abak, was sent with me all the way to Ochadamu. How's that for going the "second mile"?

My final contacts with city churches came after saying goodbye to my missionary friends, at the end of six month's visit. My new escorts, who met me at Kagoro, were Pastor Unubi and Evangelist Benjamin Adama, who calls himself my 'son' and was also my student at Ankpa before going on to Q.I.C. Bible College at Abak.

On our way north to Kaduna these men had a call to make and, as I sat waiting in the car, a woman and a young man passed by, taking an unusually long look at me. As I turned to watch them, they looked back again and before long were at my side.

"Are you Mr. Dickson?" the woman enquired.

"Yes," I replied, surprised that anyone should recognise me on this lonely road.

"I am from Idah," she said. "You knew my mother and helped her family."

She went on to tell me that she had been in America and now held a good position in Nigeria.

183

The young man was her son and she explained to him who I was. Then before leaving she slipped some money into my hand, saying, as Nigerians so often do when unable to give the visitor a gift in kind,

"Please buy something for yourself with this."

We reached our destination at 4.30 p.m., in time to attend the prayer meeting with over one hundred people present. Kaduna is another important State Capital and rail junction, famous for the Durbar, a spectacular display of horsemanship which delights foreign visitors. But I remember my stay there for quite different reasons.

The two Qua Iboe churches are over four miles apart and I was accommodated in a room next to the vestry of the one where Benjamin Adama ministers. I had a comfortable bed and all my meals brought by two members who worked in one of the hotels, so I was well looked after. On the Sunday morning I preached to an overflowing congregation of about two thousand people. A further five hundred attended the afternoon service in the other church, where a woman spoke to me whom I recognised at once as a girl who had been in Hilda's dormitory at Idah. What a joy to know that, although so far from home, she was still walking in God's way and witnessing for him.

Another lovely contact was with Dr. Ochaga and his wife Grace, who is a daughter of "Big James" Odekwe, my host in Ibaji. I had been in touch with this fine young couple when they were studying in Liverpool and was happy to visit them in their Kaduna home. What is more, when I moved on to the university city of Zaria, they surprised me by turning up in one of my meetings, just to say goodbye!

At Zaria I had a few days "off-colour" with

sickness and tiredness, but recovered quickly and was able to fulfil my engagements with leaders and members of the smaller but promising congregation there. Here, too, I found old friends, including a teacher who had worked with us at Idah.

My tour of the township churches and my visit to Nigeria ended where it began, in the international airport of Kano. Migrants from all over Nigeria find their way to this colourful and interesting city and, in order to suit all the Qua Iboe Church people, it was necessary to duplicate every class and service. This meant a busy programme with two Efik and two Igala-speaking services on the Sunday. One of my biggest thrills was to stand on the site which has been secured for the building of a Qua Iboe church in this ancient stronghold of Islam. How wonderful to serve the mighty Lord who has promised, *"I will build my church and the gates of hell shall not prevail against it."*

Friday 30th March 1979 found me once again aboard the 'plane, bound this time for Brussels, London and home. In my heart there was a song of praise and thanksgiving to my heavenly Father for his loving kindness, and for the wonderful measure of health and strength given during the past six months – and indeed, throughout my long and strenuous life. Looking down on the changing scene beneath us, I thought of the cities, villages and homes where I had seen the transformation brought by the Gospel, and I remembered the love of my Nigerian brothers and sisters in Christ, so lavishly expressed, in word and gift, to one who felt utterly unworthy.

Perhaps the event which summed it all up, and which would live most vividly in my memory, was that which had taken place in Kaduna on Thursday, 15th March. That morning I received a surprising invitation. It came from the directors of two prosperous companies, all of them Igalas, to say they had jointly arranged a dinner party in my honour for that evening. Some elders and deacons of the churches were also invited and we were asked to assemble at the hotel for 7.30 p.m.

The Durbar Hotel was a beautiful place, decorated to perfection, with shaded wall lights and tall red candles on the long table. I was given the place of honour and, after thanks to God, the uniformed waiters served soft drinks, followed by soup, delicious chicken with a choice of vegetables, fruit salad and coffee.

When the tables had been cleared, one of the guests briefly expressed their happiness to have me with them. Then the main speaker rose at the other end of the table. He was Emmanuel Abah, son of the pastor at Ogugu who was about 12 years of age when we first trekked there from Adoru. After saying many kind things which embarrassed me greatly, he continued,

"Baba, look around those who are seated at this table. These are your sons. Not one of us would have been here tonight or would have known Jesus Christ as Saviour, if you had not come with the Gospel to Igala."

He stopped and there was a stillness that said more than words. I found it hard to fight back the tears. Then he concluded,

"Baba, we rejoice to see you again and to have you with us on this memorable occasion."

It was not easy to reply, but I had to thank them for their loving thought and remind them that I was only God's messenger, commissioned by him to bring Good News to Igala. Many others, black and white, had shared in this work, but it was God alone who gave the increase. To him we must give all the glory.

After a closing prayer, many photographs were taken, and we quietly dispersed to go our several ways.

Dear friends, what more can I say? I cannot fathom why our great God should have chosen me to be his child, and given me the joyful privilege of serving him for all these years. But this I know, he keeps his promises. Has he not said,

"There is no man that hath left house, or parents, or brethren, or wife, or children, for the kingdom of God's sake, who shall not receive manifold more in this present time, and in the world to come life everlasting"?

When I left home and loved ones to sail for Nigeria in 1922, I was quite prepared to walk alone with God. Instead, he gave me a wonderful life-partner and, although we had no natural children, he raised up for us brothers and sisters, nephews and nieces, sons and daughters without number! Truly I have received manifold more in this present time. And in the world to come, what, oh what shall it be?

Life everlasting – with my Lord!

Epilogue

On a quiet Sunday morning in December 1980, the minibus collecting worshippers for the local Baptist church drew up outside No. 42 Bridgend Avenue, Port Glasgow. Usually there was a speedy response to its arrival, but today the door remained closed and the curtains drawn. Something must be wrong. A kindly neighbour had a key, and Herbert Dickson's friends entered the little house to find him sitting in his chair, unable to move after a severe stroke.

Until a few weeks previously he had been caring for his invalid sister. After her admission to hospital he had visited his relations in Northern Ireland, worked on the later chapters of this book and taken part in two Qua Iboe Mission Conferences. At the Portrush Conference, an informal hour of worship was held on the Sunday morning for those who did not feel like braving the Atlantic gale to attend a church service. Few who were present that day will forget "Uncle Herbie's" talk to the children or his meditation on the great missionary apostle's affirmation – *"I am ready . . ."* in Romans 1:15, Acts 21:13 and 2 Timothy 4:6. As he dwelt particularly on being "ready for the limitations" no one could have foreseen how soon his message would be put to the test.

Lying in a hospital bed, in weakness and discomfort, he asked the Lord to take him away home but, with characteristic honesty, he later explained to his niece,

188

"God said to me, 'My man, whose do you think you are? Don't you belong to me and hasn't your life always been safe in my hands? Surely you know me well enough to leave the end of it with me too.' What could I say but, 'True, Lord. Just help me to keep on trusting'."

Dr. Esther Davis had come home on furlough with many loving messages from friends in Nigeria who had been looking forward to seeing her uncle again in July 1981, at special services to mark the 50th anniversary of the coming of the Gospel to Igala. It was clear that he would not be able to make the journey and, realising his disappointment, she reminded him of one of his favourite promises in Romans 8:28.

"Yes," he said, "that's still true. But these days it's the first verse of the chapter that brings me greatest comfort, *'There is therefore now no condemnation to them which are in Christ Jesus.'* That's what I need to be sure of when I stand before God."

Though unable to read, his memory was so stored with Scripture that he was able to draw upon it in time of need. And he was still thinking of others.

"I'd like the book to end with a message to young people," he said. "Tell them never to hesitate to follow the Lord wherever he leads and to put him first in everything. Don't let them miss the thrill of serving him with all their heart and mind and strength."

It had been hard to decide on a title for this book. Somehow none of those already considered had seemed quite right and we wondered if he was well enough to be consulted about the latest suggestion. An opportunity came during a visit from the Mission's General Secretary, Rev. Bill Leach.

"You know the last verse of the twenty-third psalm," he said, *'Surely goodness and mercy shall follow me all the days of my life: and I will dwell in the house of the Lord for ever.'* How would you like the title for your book to be taken from that – *ALL THE DAYS OF MY LIFE?"*

There was quietness for a moment as the frail warrior thought of these familiar words. Then he said contentedly,

"That might just be it."

And so we leave God's loved and loving servant – looking back with gratitude over a full life, and looking forward with hope to a glorious future *"in the house of the Lord for ever."*

J.S.C.

The Qua Iboe Mission continues its work with the indigenous Church in Nigeria, spreading the news of God's love, justice and forgiveness through Jesus by word, literature and the practical demonstration of Christian love.

Current news is published in the Mission's magazine, *'Dispatch'*, which can be regularly received by writing to the Belfast office.

Details of home or field vacancies can also be obtained by writing to the General Secretary,

Rev. W. Leach,
Qua Iboe Mission,
Room 317,
7 Donegall Square West,
Belfast BT1 6JE,
N. Ireland.